Fashion Origami

ARCTURUS

ARCTURUS

This edition published in 2014 by Arcturus Publishing Limited
26/27 Bickels Yard, 151–153 Bermondsey Street,
London SE1 3HA

Copyright © Arcturus Holdings Limited

ISBN: 978-1-78404-060-4
CH004104NT
Supplier: 13, Date 0514, Print run 3175

Models and photography by Michael Wiles
Written by Catherine Ard
Designed by Picnic
Edited by Kate Overy and Joe Fullman

Printed in China

Contents

Tops

Summer wear

Dressing up

Accessories

Hats

Special outfits

Fashion show

Introduction

This book shows you how to create a gorgeous collection of mini fashions. All you need for each item is a square of paper, your fingers, and some clever creasing. So, forget sewing and get folding!

Getting started

The paper used in origami is thin, but strong, so that it can be folded many times. You can use ordinary scrap paper, but make sure it's not too thick.

A lot of the clothes and accessories in this book are made with the same folds. The ones that appear most are explained on these pages. It's a good idea to master these folds before you start.

Key

When making the clothes, follow this key to find out what the lines, arrows, and symbols mean.

mountain fold ··························

step fold (mountain fold and valley fold next to each other)

direction to push or pull paper ▶

valley fold – – – – – – – – –

direction to move paper

hold paper in place with finger 👉

Mountain fold

To make a mountain fold, fold the paper so that the crease is pointing up at you, like a mountain.

Valley fold

To make a valley fold, fold the paper the other way, so that the crease is pointing away from you, like a valley.

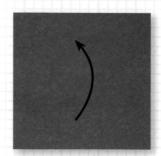

Step fold

The step fold creates a zigzag, or step, in the paper. It is used to divide different parts of a garment, such as the skirt and bodice of a dress.

1 First fold a piece of paper in half from bottom to top, then unfold.

2 Now make a mountain fold above the valley fold you just made.

3 Push the mountain fold over the valley fold and press it flat.

4 You now have a step fold.

A step fold like the one here, with the mountain fold above the valley fold, is shown like this.

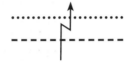

A step fold with the mountain fold below the valley fold is shown like this.

Pleat fold

Once you have mastered a step fold, making a pleat is easy. In this book, step folds are always horizontal and pleats are vertical. A pleat fold uses some creases that have been made in earlier steps.

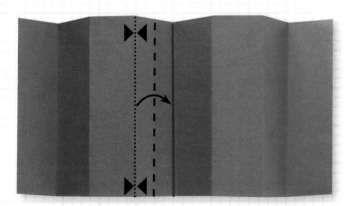 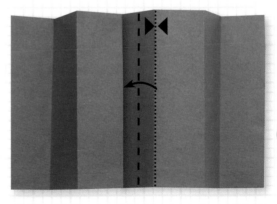

1 To make the first side of a pleat, pinch the crease shown between your fingers. Fold it over to the right until it lines up with the crease indicated. Press it flat to make a valley crease in the paper underneath.

2 Repeat on the other side. Pinch the crease shown and fold it over to the left until it lines up with the crease indicated. Press it flat to make a valley crease underneath.

Hold the paper up and the finished pleat will look like this from the side.

Tops

An easy way to change your outfit is to get a new top! Choose from long and hippy, fitted and pretty, short and flared, or simple and sporty. Take your pick to suit your mood!

Ship ahoy!

Sailor top

Sports shirt

Anyone for tennis?

Crop top

Blouse

Swing your thing!

Smock top

Crop top

Fold this fun, short shirt and you can rock a crop without ever needing to bare your belly!

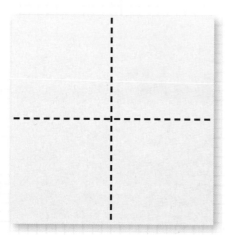

1. Fold the paper top to bottom and unfold. Then left to right and unfold.

2. Fold the edges in to meet the central crease.

3. Make two angled folds from a finger's width below the middle to the bottom corners. These will be the sleeves.

4. Valley fold the paper at the top of the angled folds you just made.

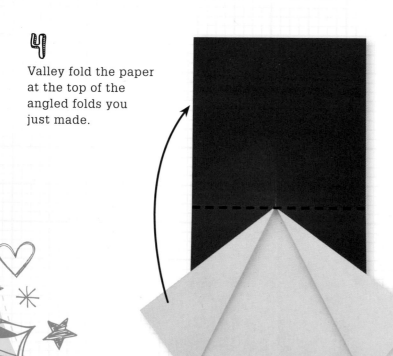

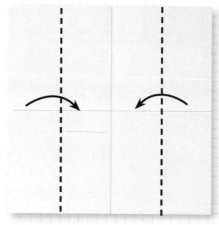

5. For the collar, make angled creases from the top corners to the middle of the paper.

6

Turn the paper over.

7

Valley fold the corners so that they meet on the central crease.

8

When you have this shape, turn the paper over.

9

Mountain fold the top of the collar as shown.

10

Your crop top is complete. It's cool for the summer and definitely different!

Sports shirt

Get in training with this fab sports shirt. Warm up with a few simple folds and creases and before you know it, it'll be game, set, and match!

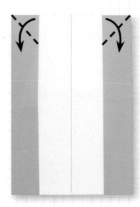

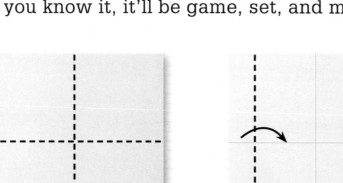

1 Fold the paper top to bottom and unfold. Then left to right and unfold.

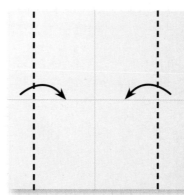

2 Fold in the sides 25 mm (1 in) from either edge. Mark a faint line to help, if you like.

3 Valley fold the top corners to line up with the outside edges.

4 Fold in the edges to meet the central crease.

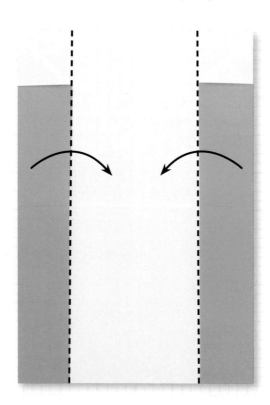

5 To make the collar, make two angled folds that meet in a 'V' in the middle as shown.

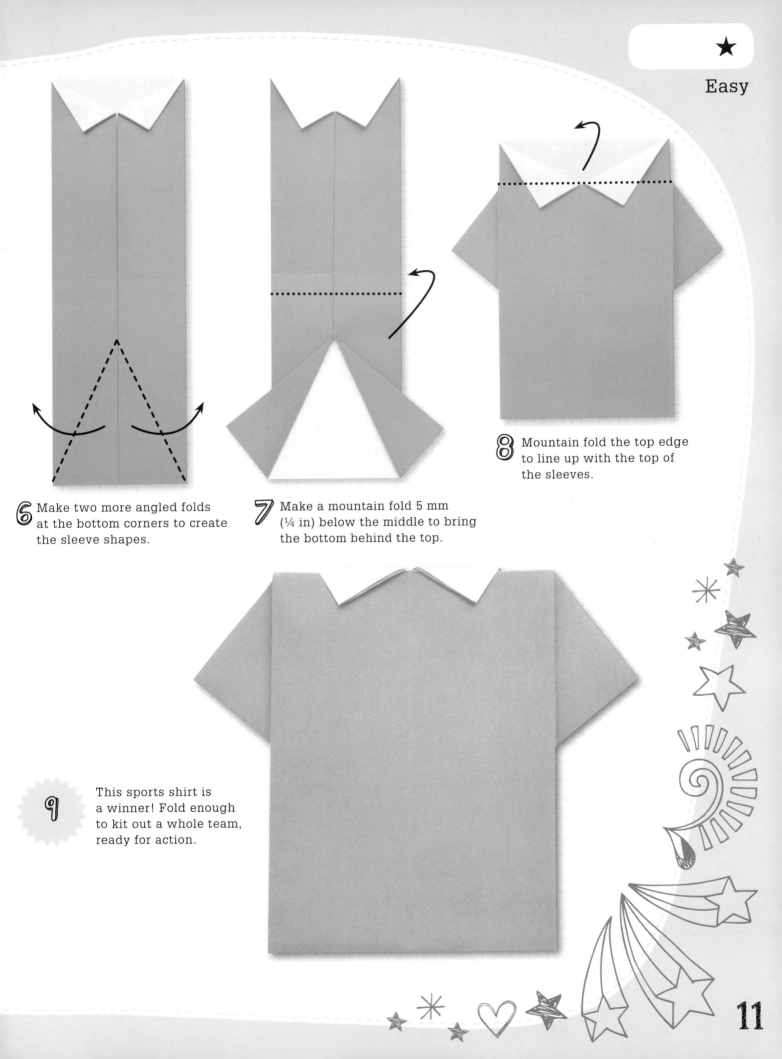

6 Make two more angled folds at the bottom corners to create the sleeve shapes.

7 Make a mountain fold 5 mm (¼ in) below the middle to bring the bottom behind the top.

8 Mountain fold the top edge to line up with the top of the sleeves.

9 This sports shirt is a winner! Fold enough to kit out a whole team, ready for action.

Smock top

Make a swinging smock top with plenty of Sixties style. Pick a strong shade to make the white neck and border really pop!

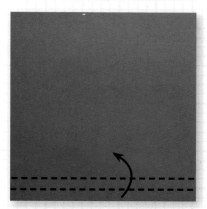

1 Make a valley fold 5 mm (¼ in) from the bottom edge and fold it over twice to reveal a white strip.

2 Turn the paper over.

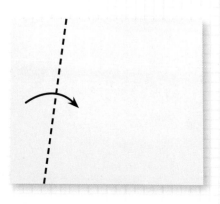

3 Make an angled crease on the left side around 50 mm (2 in) from the edge at the top.

4 Fold back the corner as shown.

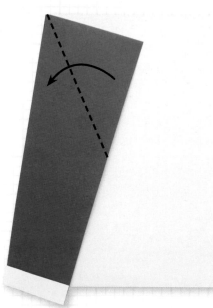

5 Now make an angled crease on the right side. Check that it matches the fold you made on the left side.

6 Fold back the corner as shown.

7 Turn the paper over.

8 Valley fold the top around 10 mm (½ in) from the edge.

9 Make two mountain folds at the bottom to hide the untidy corners.

10 Swing your thing with your trendy smock top. All it needs is a matching bag and some spiky Sixties shoes.

Sailor top

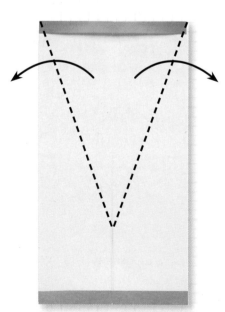

Ahoy there! This stylish boating top will add some fun to your paper fashions. Choose a bright ocean blue and set sail for the high seas!

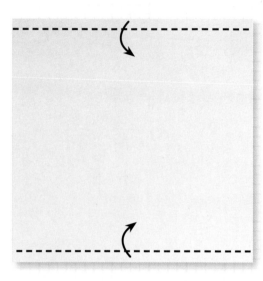

1 Valley fold a narrow section on the top and bottom edges.

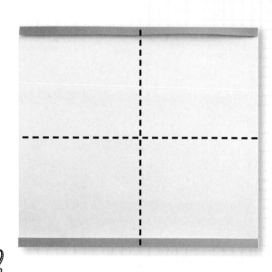

2 Fold the paper in half from top to bottom and unfold. Then fold it from left to right and unfold. Turn the paper over.

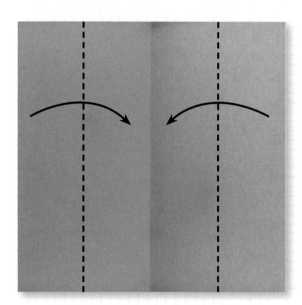

3 Fold the edges in to meet the central crease.

4 Make two angled folds from the top corners that meet in a 'V' around 30 mm (1½ in) below the middle. This will shape the sleeves and the collar.

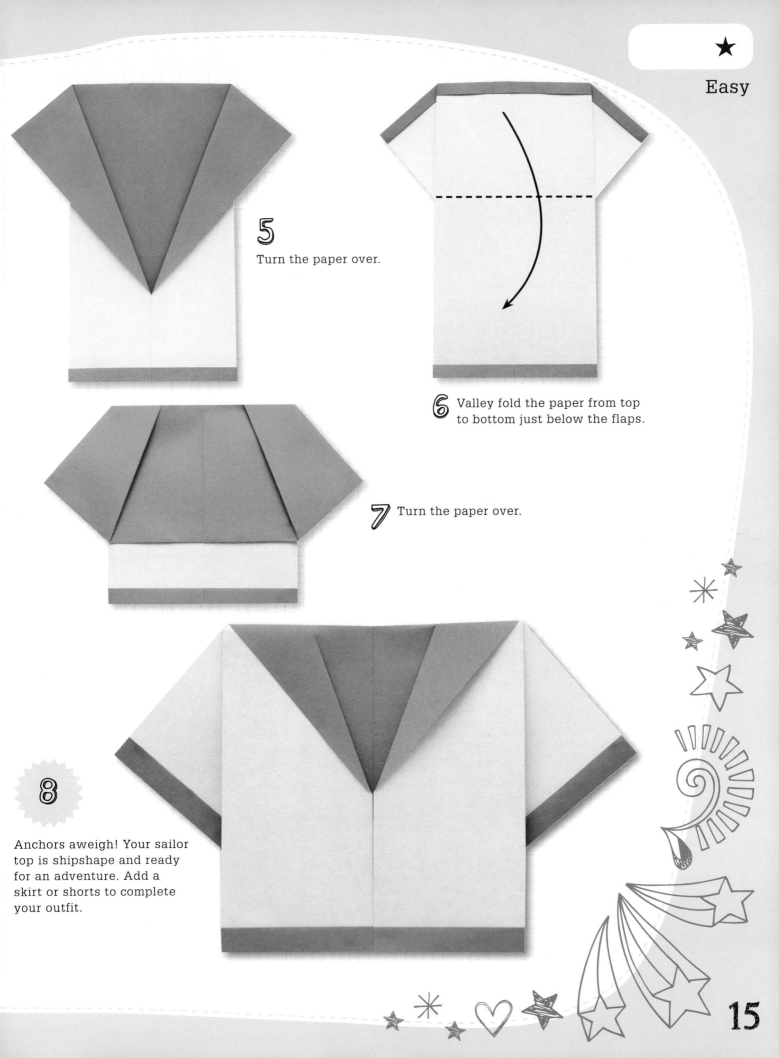

5 Turn the paper over.

6 Valley fold the paper from top to bottom just below the flaps.

7 Turn the paper over.

8 Anchors aweigh! Your sailor top is shipshape and ready for an adventure. Add a skirt or shorts to complete your outfit.

Blouse

Step out in style with this cute, short-sleeved blouse. Choose a pretty pink or pastel paper and follow the steps to fold a dainty collar and cuffs.

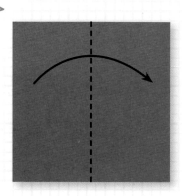

1 Fold the paper in half from left to right.

2 Fold in a 10 mm (½ in) section on both edges.

3 Turn the paper over.

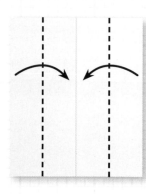

4 Fold the edges in to meet the central crease.

5

Make two angled creases as shown. When folded over the edges should be straight.

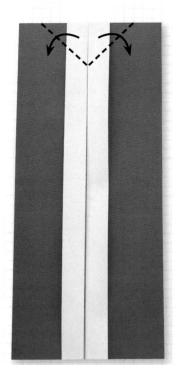

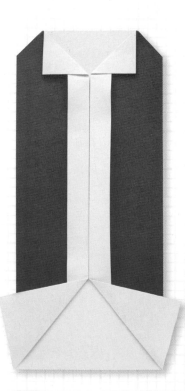

6 Shape the shoulders with mountain folds. Now make angled creases from the bottom corners.

7 Turn the paper over.

16

9 Unfold the two white flaps.

10 Valley fold the sides as shown.

8 Valley fold the paper from bottom to top. The edge should meet the bottom of the corner folds.

11 Fold over these new flaps with two vertical creases from the bottom corners.

12 Fold down the upper flaps again along their original creases.

13 Turn the paper over to see the full effect.

14 One freshly folded blouse ready to wear. Pair it with a pleated skirt in a matching shade for a gorgeously girlie look.

Summer wear

Get ready for the summer with a cool collection of outfits. There's something for every sunny occasion, from picnics to pool parties!

T-shirt

Summer dress

Let's have a barbecue!

Shorts

Swimsuit

Pinafore

Pleated Skirt

Fancy a dip?

I've packed a picnic!

T-shirt and shorts

Fold a pair of easy shorts and a comfy T-shirt. It's the perfect outfit for hot summer days. Co-ordinate the top and shorts, or mix and match different papers.

T-SHIRT

1 Fold the paper from left to right and unfold. Then fold it top to bottom and unfold.

2 Fold in the edges to meet the central crease.

3 Valley fold a narrow section on both edges so a white strip is showing.

4 Make the sleeves with two angled creases from the middle of the inside edges to the bottom corners.

5 Valley fold the paper in half from the bottom to the top. Now your T-shirt is nearly finished.

6 Turn the paper over and press down firmly on the creases. Your crisp, new T-shirt is ready for the next sunny day!

SHORTS

1 Follow steps 1 and 2 for T-shirt, then unfold the paper. Fold the bottom edge in, as shown.

2 Turn the paper over.

3 Make angled creases from the bottom corners to the first crease along the top edge on either side.

4 Fold in one side, pressing down firmly. Repeat on the other side. These will be the legs.

5 Mountain fold the top half of the paper behind the bottom half.

6 Check the folded half does not show below the white strip. Make a crease 10 mm (½ in) from the top edge.

7 Fold down along the new crease and press firmly to make the waistband. Your shorts are finished!

8 Now team your shorts up with your T-shirt. What could be cooler on a hot summer day?

Swimsuit

Make a splash on sunny days with a cute swimsuit that's easy to fold. Blend in at the beach with ocean blue, or stand out at the pool with a zingy shade.

1 Fold the paper in half from top to bottom and unfold. Then from left to right and unfold.

2 Fold the paper in half from top to bottom once more.

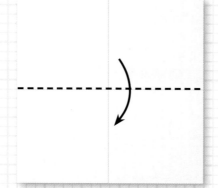

3 Fold the bottom corners up to meet in the middle of the top edge.

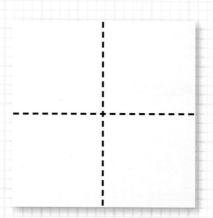

4 You should now have a triangle. Unfold the last two folds.

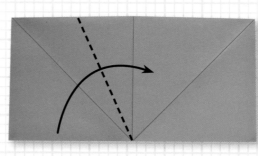

5 Fold the left side over so the bottom edge meets the diagonal crease on the opposite side.

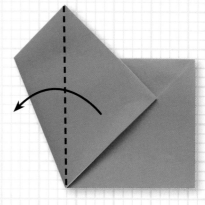

6 Valley fold the paper along the original fold to make a triangle.

7 Repeat steps 5 and 6 on the other side. You can open out the paper to check the bottom edge meets the diagonal crease on the opposite side.

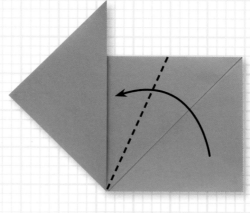

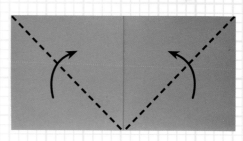

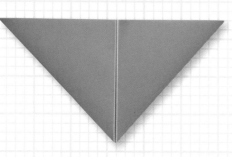

8 You should have two triangles that meet to form a square. Make two angled creases at the top.

9 Fold down, making sure the bottom edges are straight and the outer edges line up, then unfold.

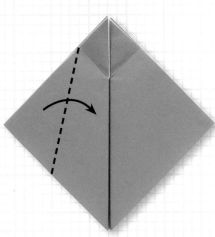

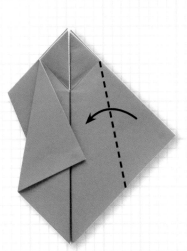

10 Valley fold the left side from the edge of the crease, as shown.

11 Repeat on the right side.

12 Your paper should look like this. Turn the paper over.

13 Mountain fold the top corners along the creases that you made before. Press down firmly.

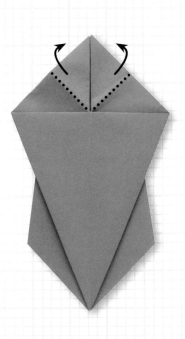

14 Your strapless swimsuit is ready for a dip. Time to grab the sunscreen and hit the beach!

Pleated skirt

When it comes to paper fashions, pleats are totally neat, so get folding to make an easy, pleated skirt that's stylish too!

1 Make a fold around 5 mm (¼ in) from the top edge so a white strip is showing.

2 Turn the paper over, keeping the white strip at the top.

3 Fold the paper in half from left to right.

4 Crease firmly, then unfold the paper again.

5 Fold the paper in half from top to bottom.

6 Fold the edges in to meet the central crease.

7 Repeat step 6, folding the edges in to meet the central crease.

8 Your paper should look like this. Unfold the paper, keeping the white strip at the bottom.

9 Turn the paper over.

10 Now make the first pleat. Take the third crease from the left to meet the central crease. Press it flat.

11 Repeat step 10 on the other side, taking the third crease from the right to meet the central crease. Press it flat.

12 You should now have a pleat down the middle of the paper.

It should look like this from the side. Turn the paper over.

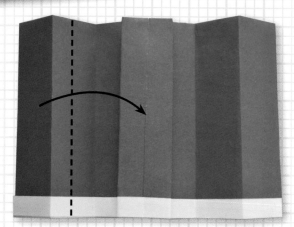

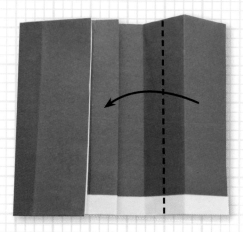

13 With the white strip along the bottom, fold the left edge in to meet the central crease.

14 Then fold the right edge in to meet the central crease.

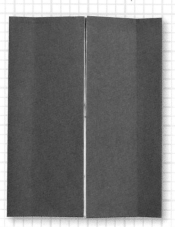

15 Unfold both sides, making sure that the pleat you made is still in place.

16 Turn the paper over, keeping the white strip at the bottom.

17

Now make another pleat. Take the second crease from the left and fold it over along the third crease.

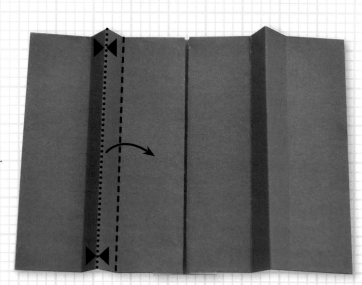

18 Repeat step 17 on the other side, taking the second crease from the right and folding it over along the third crease.

19 Make a valley fold from the first crease on the top edge to the bottom corner.

20 Make a matching fold on the other side to create the flared shape of the skirt.

21 Fold down the top 10 mm (½ in) of the skirt to hide the open edges. Your skirt is nearly ready.

22 Press down firmly along the top to crease the pleated layers, then turn the paper over.

23 Ta-da! One neatly pleated skirt, complete with a pretty band, ready to swing into action!

Summer dress

It takes just a few minutes of folding to create this fabulous, bright summer dress. Use different papers to create a whole summer wardrobe.

1 Fold the paper left to right and unfold. Then fold it top to bottom and unfold.

2 Make a valley crease in the bottom half of the paper.

3 Fold the bottom edge of the paper up to the central crease, then unfold.

4 Make another crease halfway between the bottom of the paper and the valley crease.

5 Fold the bottom of the paper up to the new crease, so a section of white is showing.

6 Turn the paper over and fold the edges in to meet the central crease.

7 Make a step fold halfway between the top and the white strip at the bottom.

8 Press down on the step fold so it lies flat. Turn the paper over.

28

9 Make two angled creases in the middle edge, as shown.

10 Fold along the creases to make two triangular shapes.

11 Make a new fold from the triangle tip to the bottom corner. Press down on the crease, as shown.

12 Repeat on the other side, folding from the tip of the triangle to the bottom corner. Press down on the top crease as shown.

13 Fold in the edges so they meet at the central crease.

14 Make two new creases in the top section as shown.

15 Turn the paper over. Your dress is nearly complete.

16 To make the neck, make two new angled creases that meet in a 'V' in the middle.

17 Fold along the creases, making sure the bottom edges are straight. Your new dress is now ready for that important summer party!

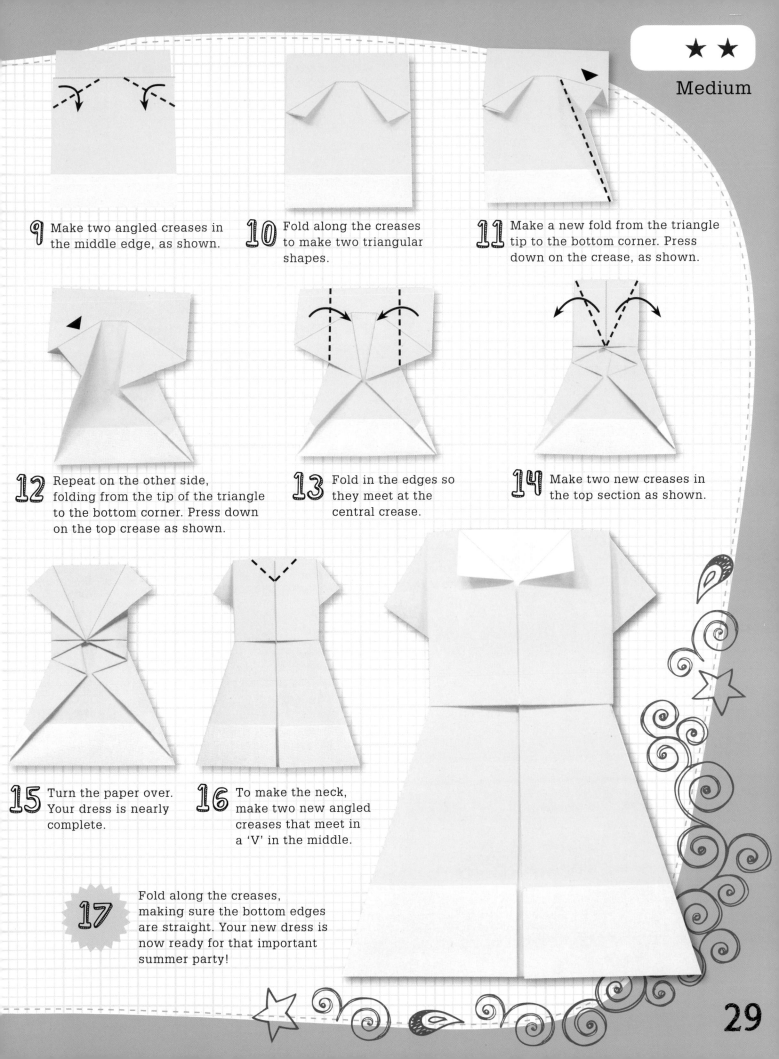

Pinafore

This pretty, everyday pinafore dress is a must for every girl's summer wardrobe. Pair it with a T-shirt, or keep it simple and strappy.

1 Fold the paper in half from top to bottom and unfold. Then from left to right and unfold.

2 Fold the edges in to meet the central crease.

3 Unfold the paper.

4 Fold in both sides about 10 mm (½ in) from the edge.

5 Mountain fold the sides along the creases that you made earlier.

6 Make a new crease about 25 mm (1 in) from the top edge.

7 Fold down the paper and crease firmly.

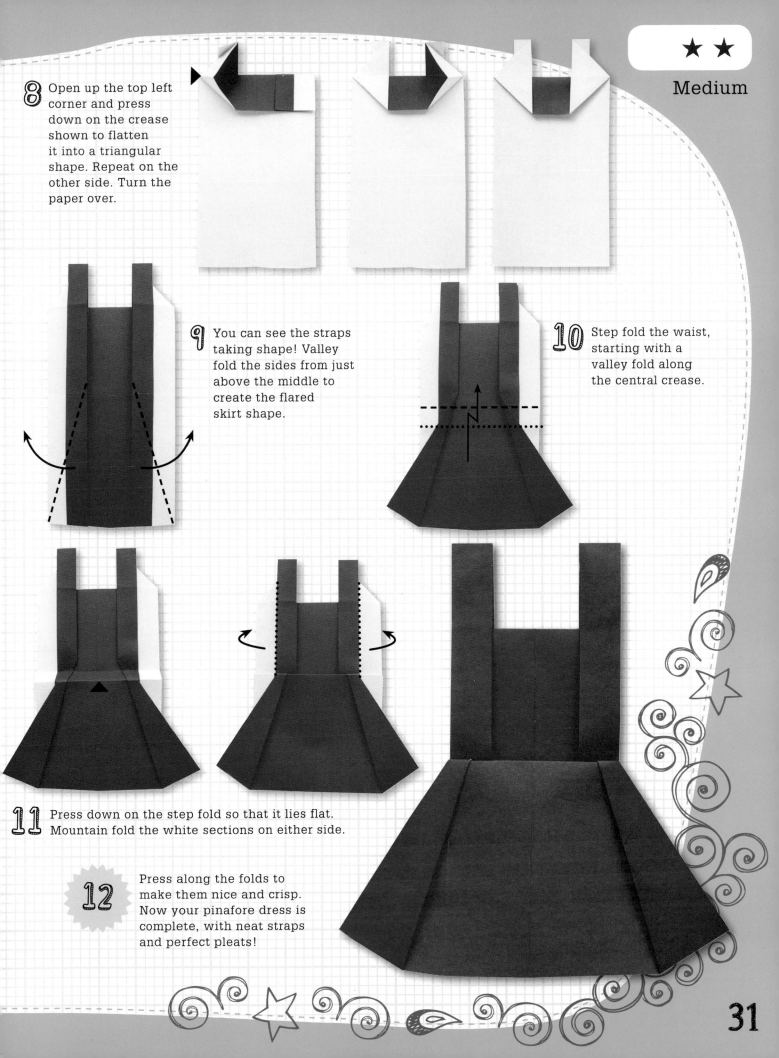

8 Open up the top left corner and press down on the crease shown to flatten it into a triangular shape. Repeat on the other side. Turn the paper over.

9 You can see the straps taking shape! Valley fold the sides from just above the middle to create the flared skirt shape.

10 Step fold the waist, starting with a valley fold along the central crease.

11 Press down on the step fold so that it lies flat. Mountain fold the white sections on either side.

12 Press along the folds to make them nice and crisp. Now your pinafore dress is complete, with neat straps and perfect pleats!

Dressing up

This collection really is super-stylish! Fold some fabulous evening wear for glittering parties and glamorous dinner dates.

Let's dance!

Kick up your heels!

Party dress

Evening gown

May I take your coat?

Smart suit

Dress coat

High heels

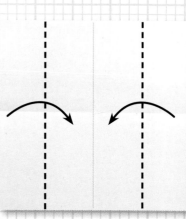

Make your creases extra sharp and your folds totally faultless for this snappy two-piece suit.

PART 1

1 Fold the paper in half from top to bottom and unfold. Then from left to right and unfold.

2 Mountain fold a narrow strip on the top edge. This will be the sleeve cuffs.

3 Fold the edges in to meet the central crease.

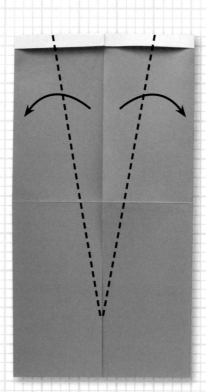

4 Make two angled creases that meet in a 'V' as shown. When folded back, the tips of the flaps should meet the edges of the paper.

5 Turn the paper over.

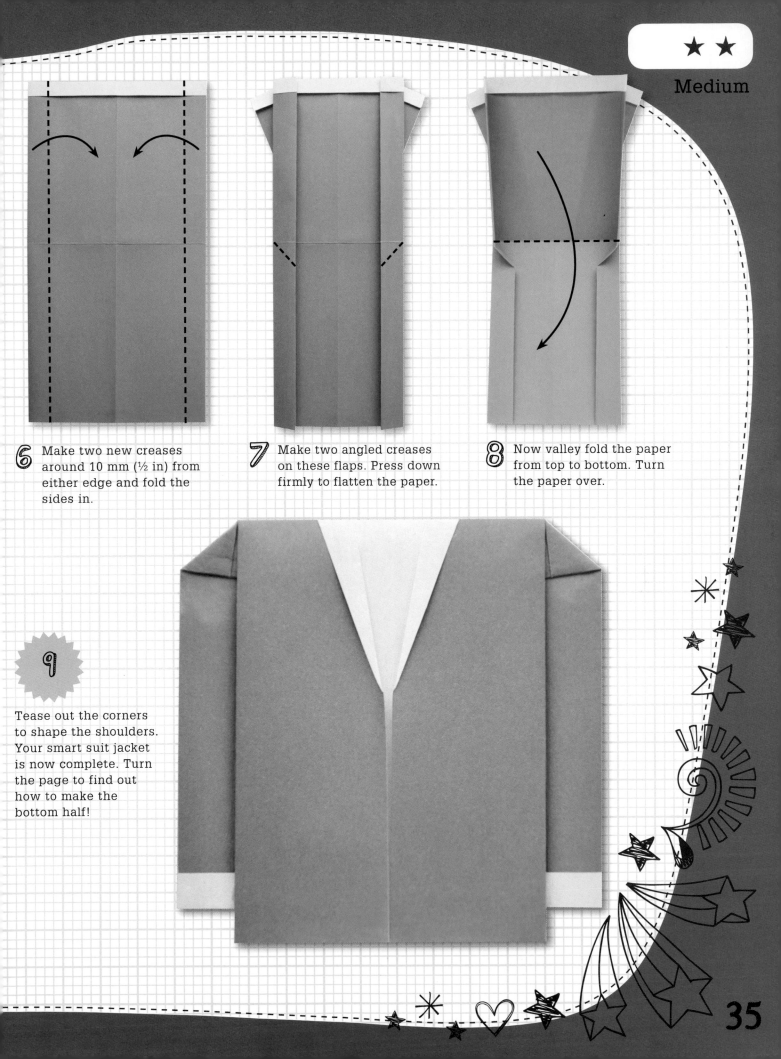

6 Make two new creases around 10 mm (½ in) from either edge and fold the sides in.

7 Make two angled creases on these flaps. Press down firmly to flatten the paper.

8 Now valley fold the paper from top to bottom. Turn the paper over.

9 Tease out the corners to shape the shoulders. Your smart suit jacket is now complete. Turn the page to find out how to make the bottom half!

Smart suit

PART 2

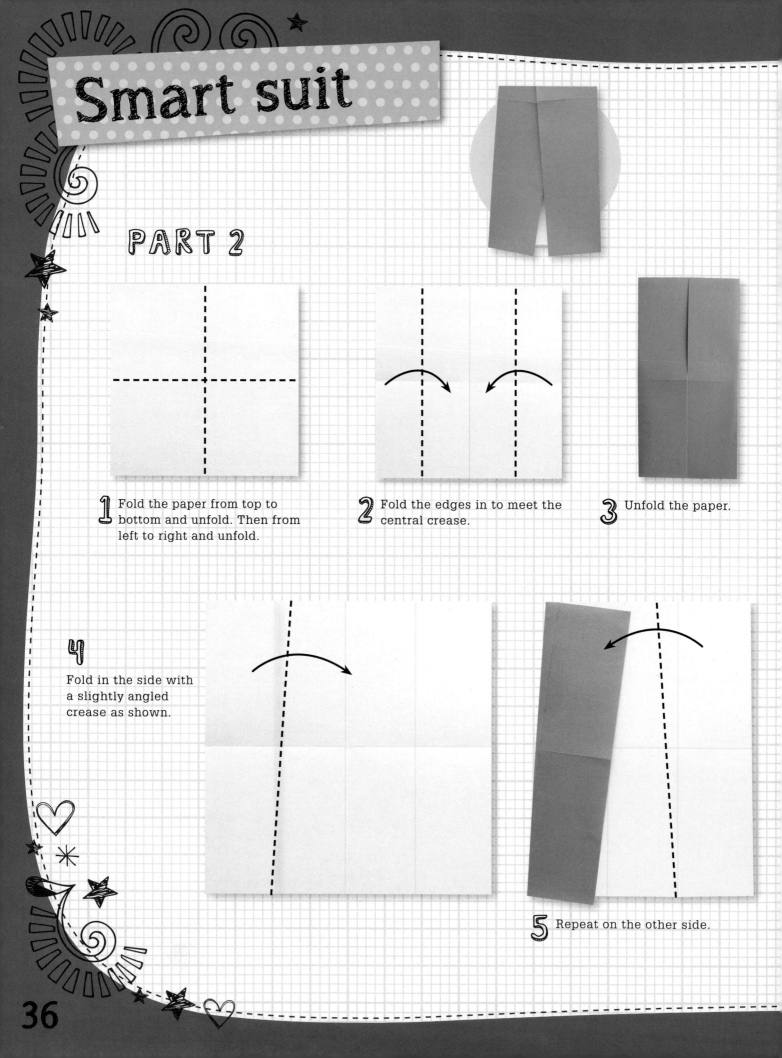

1 Fold the paper from top to bottom and unfold. Then from left to right and unfold.

2 Fold the edges in to meet the central crease.

3 Unfold the paper.

4 Fold in the side with a slightly angled crease as shown.

5 Repeat on the other side.

6 Mountain fold the edges at the same slight angle.

7 Mountain fold the top as shown.

8 Now the two parts of your suit are pressed and ready. Put them together and you have one stylish outfit all set for a dinner date!

High heels

What could be more elegant than a brand new pair of high heels? Fold these right and they'll stand up on their own.

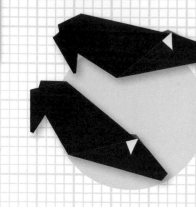

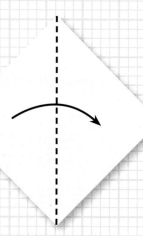

1 Place the paper as shown. Make a crease down the middle, then unfold.

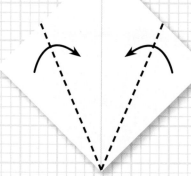

2 Make two diagonal creases from halfway along the top edges to the bottom middle.

3 Fold in one side, making sure the top edge is straight. Repeat on the other side.

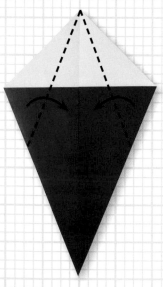

4 Make two new creases as shown by folding in the side points to the central crease.

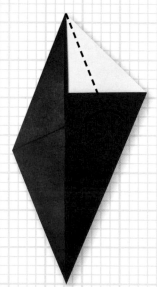

5 Fold one side into the central crease to make a triangle shape. Repeat on the other side.

6 Make two new creases in the triangles you have just made. Line up with the outside edges.

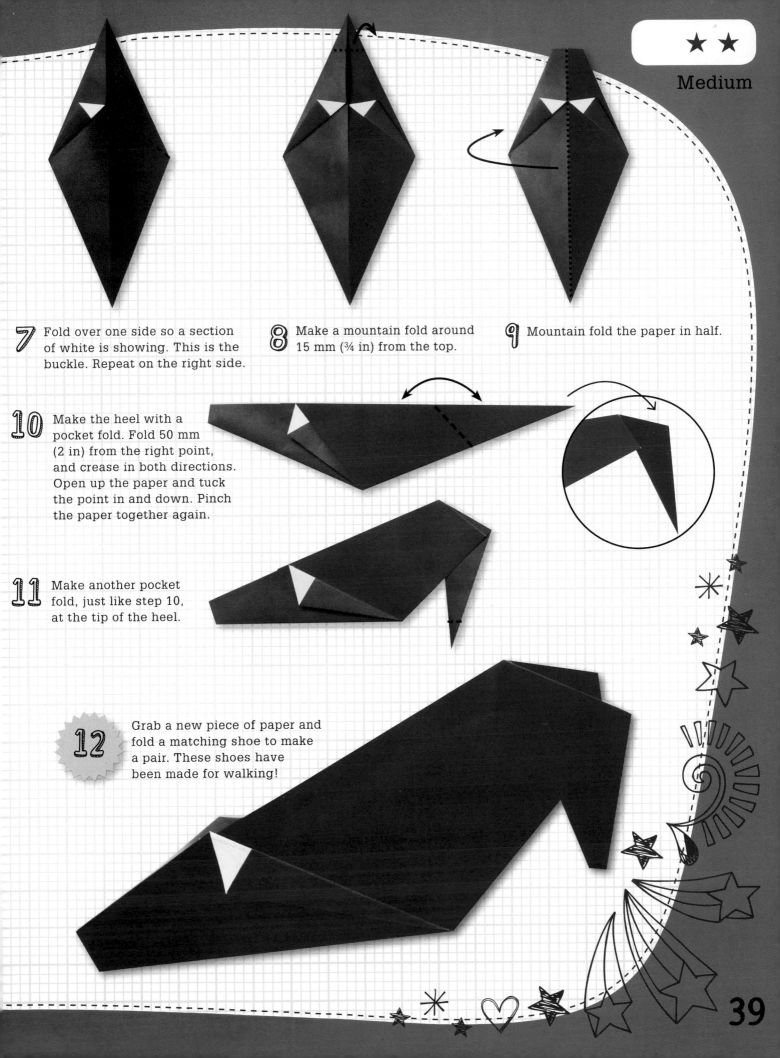

7 Fold over one side so a section of white is showing. This is the buckle. Repeat on the right side.

8 Make a mountain fold around 15 mm (¾ in) from the top.

9 Mountain fold the paper in half.

10 Make the heel with a pocket fold. Fold 50 mm (2 in) from the right point, and crease in both directions. Open up the paper and tuck the point in and down. Pinch the paper together again.

11 Make another pocket fold, just like step 10, at the tip of the heel.

12 Grab a new piece of paper and fold a matching shoe to make a pair. These shoes have been made for walking!

Dress coat

Fold this classy coat to wear over a party dress or a long evening gown. It's the perfect way to keep out the cold on chilly nights on the town.

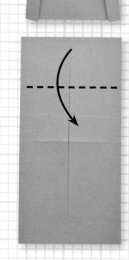

1 Fold the paper from top to bottom and unfold. Then from left to right and unfold.

2 Fold in the edges to meet the central crease.

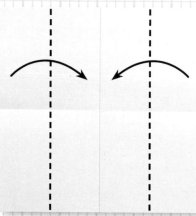

3 Now fold down the top edge to meet the central crease.

4 Turn the paper over.

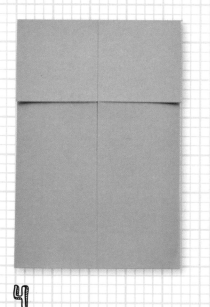

5 Make an angled crease on either side and fold in the edges.

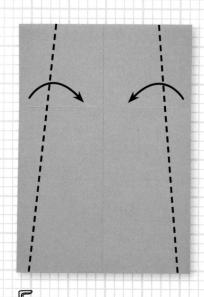

6 Hold down the lower part of the left-hand flap with your finger and open up the top corner.

7 Press down on the crease on the top edge and flatten the paper to make a triangular shape. This is a sleeve and collar!

8 Repeat on the other side. Try to make the points of the collar match.

9 Mountain fold a narrow strip along the edges of the sleeves.

10 Your stylish new coat is ready. Don't forget your party invitation on your way out the door. TAXI!

Party dress

Finding the perfect dress for a party couldn't be easier! With its tiny waist and full, swishing skirt, this one is sure to be a hit on the dance floor.

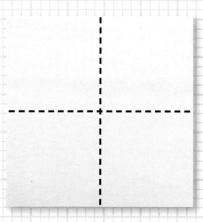

1 Fold the paper from top to bottom and unfold. Then from left to right and unfold.

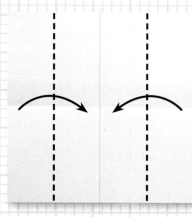

2 Fold in the edges to meet the central crease.

3 Open out the paper and turn it over.

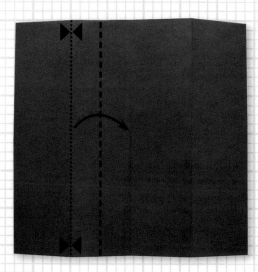

4 Now make a pleat. Take the crease on the left to meet the central crease.

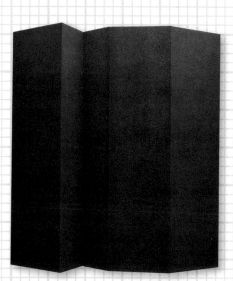

5 Press flat to crease the paper underneath.

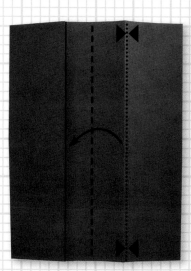

6 Repeat on the other side, taking the crease on the right to meet the central. Press flat.

7 You should now have a pleat down the middle of the paper, like this. Turn the paper over.

8 Step fold the paper from top to bottom around 5 mm (¼ in) above the central crease.

9 Press down on the step fold so that it lies flat. Turn the paper over.

10 Put your finger where the edges meet and pull the pleat to the side to reveal the paper underneath.

11 Press down on the top crease as shown to make a new angled crease. Repeat on the other side.

12 Make two angled creases at the top that meet in a 'V' in the middle. Make sure the bottom edges are straight.

13 Unfold these new creases.

14 Turn the paper over.

15 Make a valley fold 15 mm (¾ in) from the top edge.

16 Unfold the new crease.

17 Open up the pleat and place your finger on it. Press down on the crease as shown. Flatten the paper to make a triangular shape. Repeat on the other side.

18 Valley fold the left side on the upper section as shown.

19 The lower section will be pulled across. Press down on it to make an angled crease. This creates the flared shape of the skirt.

20

Repeat on the other side, folding in the upper section and making an angled crease on the lower section.

21 Valley fold the upper sections from the outer to the inner corners to make the sleeves.

22 Turn the paper over to see the finished dress.

23

This frock is ready to rock! Perfect for twirling the night away or sitting prettily at the side.

Evening gown

This dazzling evening gown is made for glittering balls and glamorous parties. Choose midnight blue or deep purple for a totally elegant look.

1 Fold the paper from top to bottom and unfold. Then from left to right and unfold.

2 Fold the edges in to meet the central crease.

3 Fold the edges in again to meet the central crease.

4 Completely unfold the paper. Turn the paper over.

5 Now make a pleat. Take the second crease from the left to meet the central crease. Fold flat.

6 Repeat on the other side, taking the second crease from the right to meet the central crease. Fold flat.

7 You should have a neat pleat down the middle of the paper. Turn the paper over.

8 Now to make the neck. Valley fold the middle section around 10 mm (½ in) from the top edge.

9 Open up the pleat and place your finger on it. Pull the left corner up and press down to make an angled crease as shown. Repeat on the other side.

Evening gown

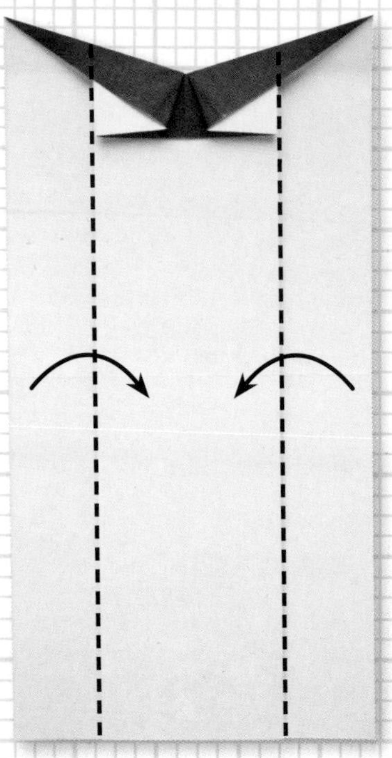

10

Fold in the left and right edges to meet the central crease.

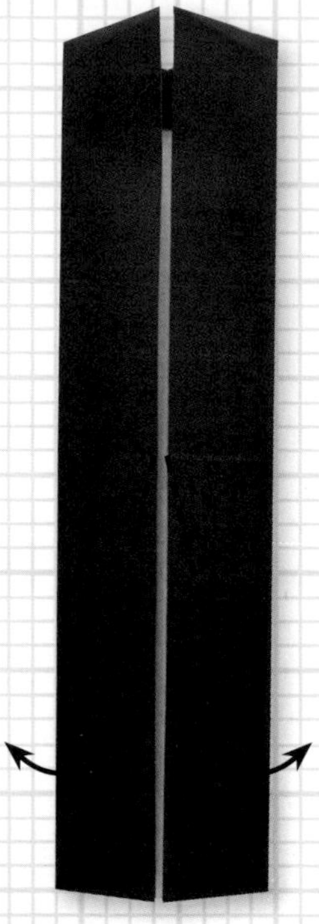

11

Make angled creases from the middle to the bottom corners. This is the skirt.

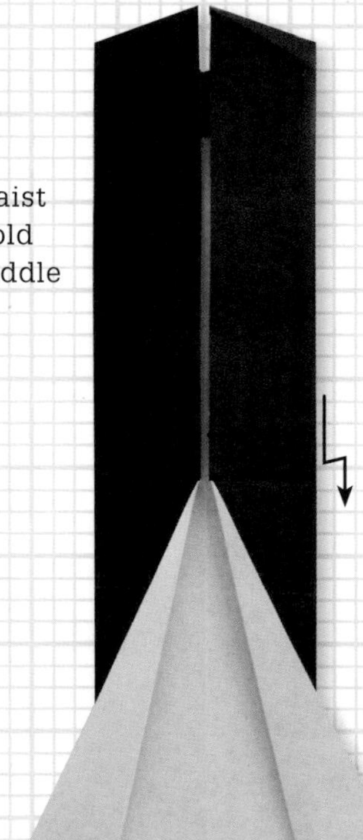

12

Create the waist with a step fold across the middle of the paper.

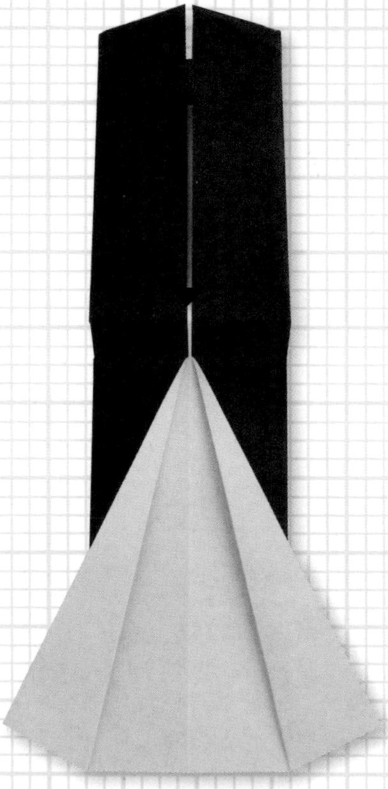

13

Press down on the step fold so that it lies flat.

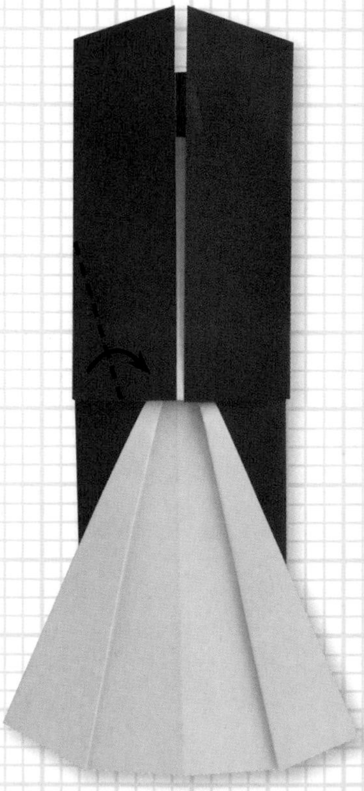

14

Now to shape the waist. First make an angled crease on the upper section.

15 Repeat on the other side.

16 Pinch the corner between your fingers and fold it over.

17 Press down firmly on the edge of the lower section to make a new crease. Repeat on the other side.

18 Turn the paper over to see the finished dress.

19 This gorgeous evening gown is ready to sweep down the red carpet.

Accessories

Pick the perfect accessories to match your paper outfits, whatever the weather. There are cool shades and warm mittens, boots, bags, and even some paper bling!

Clutch bag

Necktie

Hey, dude!

Sunglasses

Mittens

Let it snow!

Socks

Bangle

Nice boots!

Boots

Necktie

There are no tricky knots to master with this origami necktie. Follow the simple steps and you will have a fantastic result in minutes!

1
Place the paper as shown. Fold it in half from left to right and unfold.

2
Fold in the left and right edges from the top corner to meet the central crease.

3
Now you have a kite shape. Turn the paper over.

4
Valley fold the top so that the point lines up with the points on either side.

5
Fold up the tip as shown.

6
Make a crease just above the tip and fold the paper up once more.

7

Make two small angled creases on either side as shown.

8

Turn the paper over.

9

Fold in the left and right edges to meet the middle. Crease firmly over the layers at the top.

10

Turn the paper over.

11

Your necktie is now ready! Try drawing on a pattern of spots or stripes with a felt-tip pen to give your necktie some extra style.

Sunglasses

Keep your cool with these designer sunglasses. It only takes a few easy folds and a lot of rolls to create these trendy wrap-around shades.

1 Place the paper as shown and fold it in half from top to bottom.

2 Taking the top layer only, fold in the tip of the bottom corner around 15 mm (¾ in) from the point.

3 Make a crease around 10 mm (½ in) from the top edge. Fold the paper over, keeping it straight.

4 Roll the paper over, creasing the paper next to the fold you just made.

5 Roll and crease the paper again in the same way. Press down firmly after each roll.

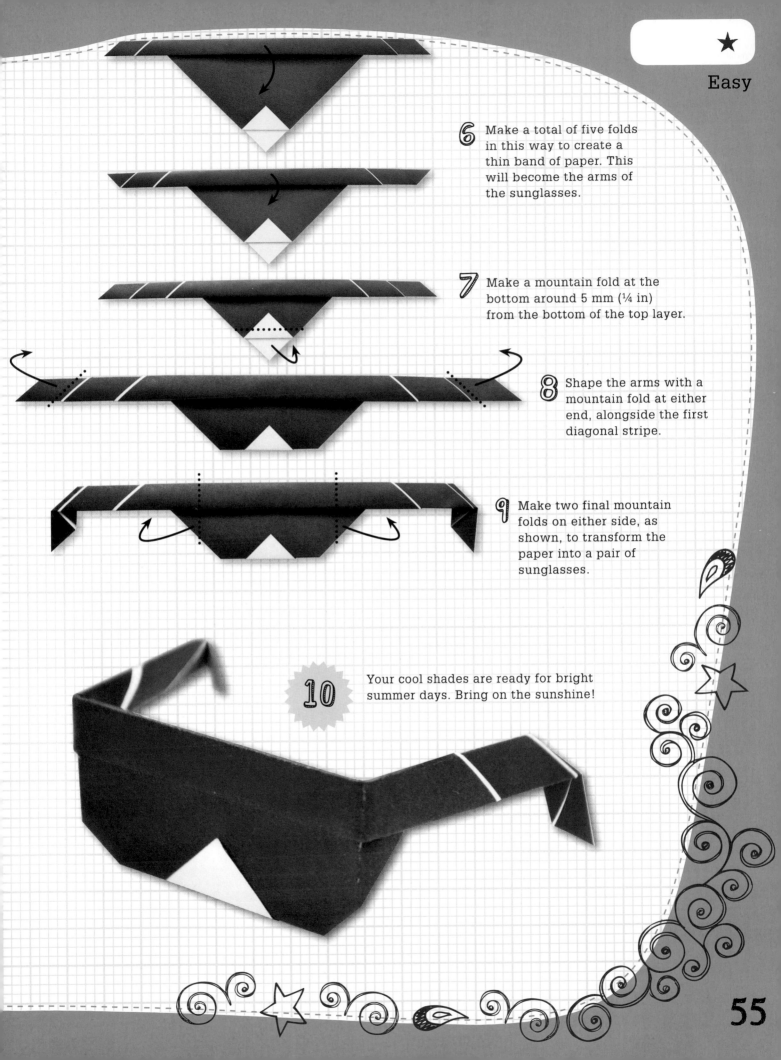

6 Make a total of five folds in this way to create a thin band of paper. This will become the arms of the sunglasses.

7 Make a mountain fold at the bottom around 5 mm (¼ in) from the bottom of the top layer.

8 Shape the arms with a mountain fold at either end, alongside the first diagonal stripe.

9 Make two final mountain folds on either side, as shown, to transform the paper into a pair of sunglasses.

10 Your cool shades are ready for bright summer days. Bring on the sunshine!

Clutch bag

Fold a cute clutch with bags of style. It's handy and neat, and perfect for holding all those important items, such as money, lipstick, and a mirror.

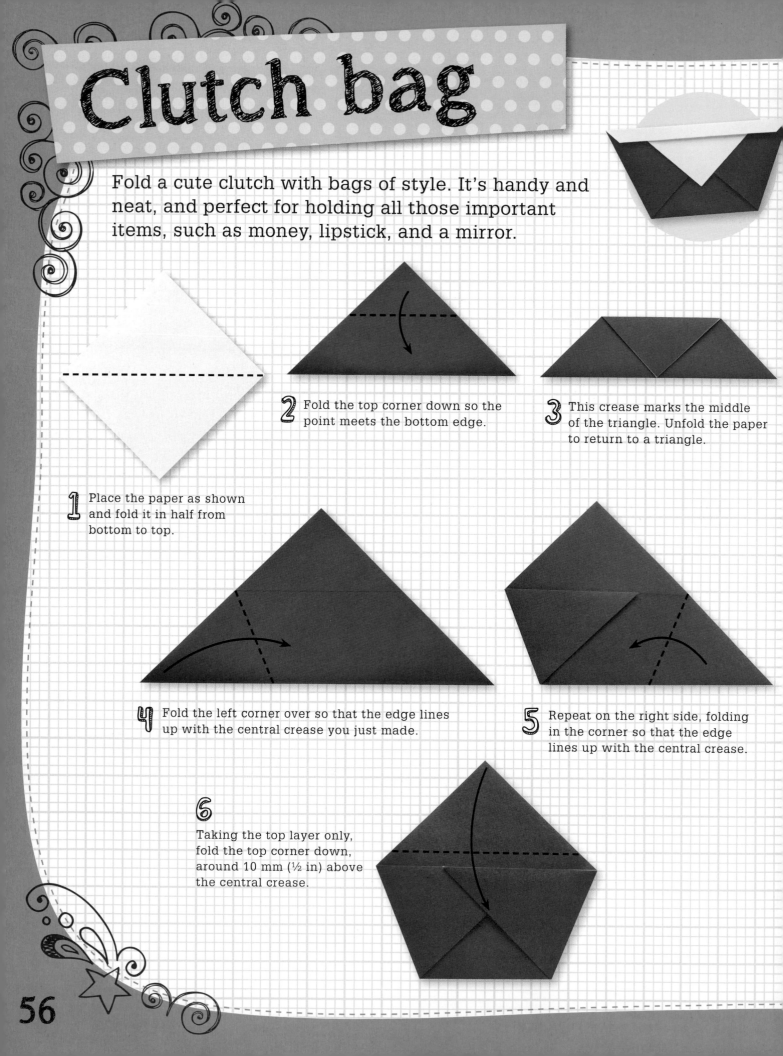

1 Place the paper as shown and fold it in half from bottom to top.

2 Fold the top corner down so the point meets the bottom edge.

3 This crease marks the middle of the triangle. Unfold the paper to return to a triangle.

4 Fold the left corner over so that the edge lines up with the central crease you just made.

5 Repeat on the right side, folding in the corner so that the edge lines up with the central crease.

6 Taking the top layer only, fold the top corner down, around 10 mm (½ in) above the central crease.

56

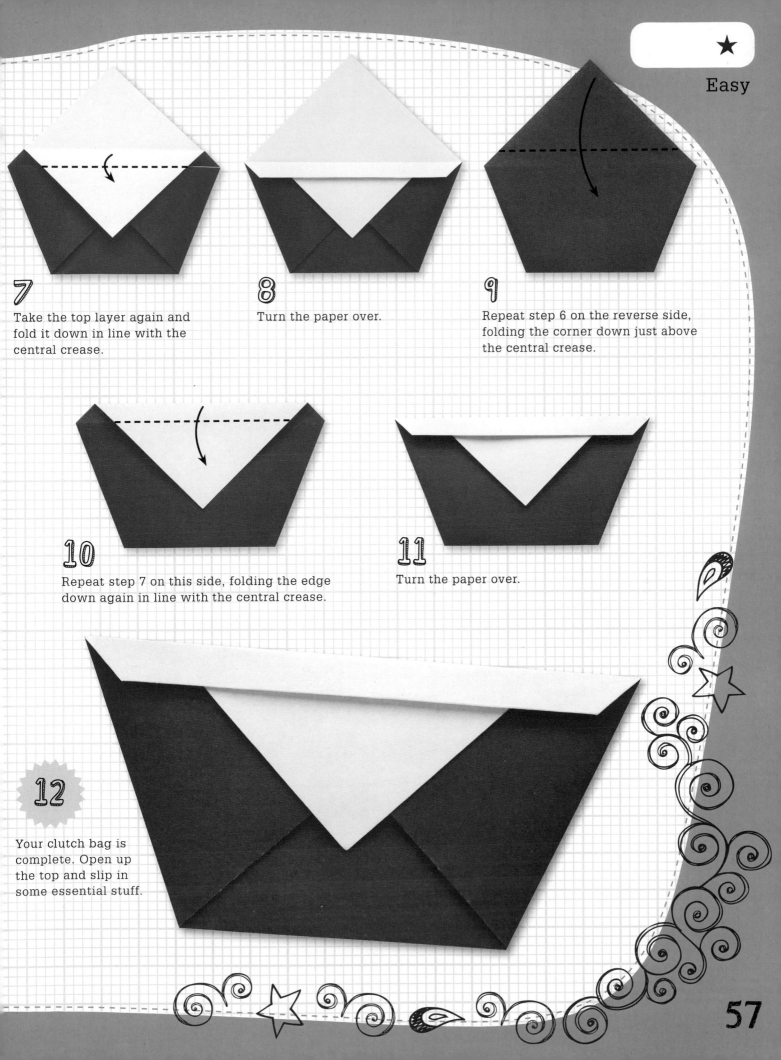

7 Take the top layer again and fold it down in line with the central crease.

8 Turn the paper over.

9 Repeat step 6 on the reverse side, folding the corner down just above the central crease.

10 Repeat step 7 on this side, folding the edge down again in line with the central crease.

11 Turn the paper over.

12 Your clutch bag is complete. Open up the top and slip in some essential stuff.

Bangle

Get ready to roll a fab bangle without the jingle-jangle. Choose a bright paper to create really dazzling diagonal stripes.

1 Place the paper as shown. Fold it in half from top to bottom and unfold, then from left to right and unfold.

2 Valley fold the paper from bottom to top, leaving a 5 mm (¼ in) border of white around the top edges.

3 Turn the paper over.

4 Fold the bottom edge in again with a valley fold 5 mm (¼ in) above the central crease.

5 Roll the paper over, creasing the paper next to the fold you just made.

6 Roll over and crease again. You can see the pattern of diagonal stripes beginning to appear at either end.

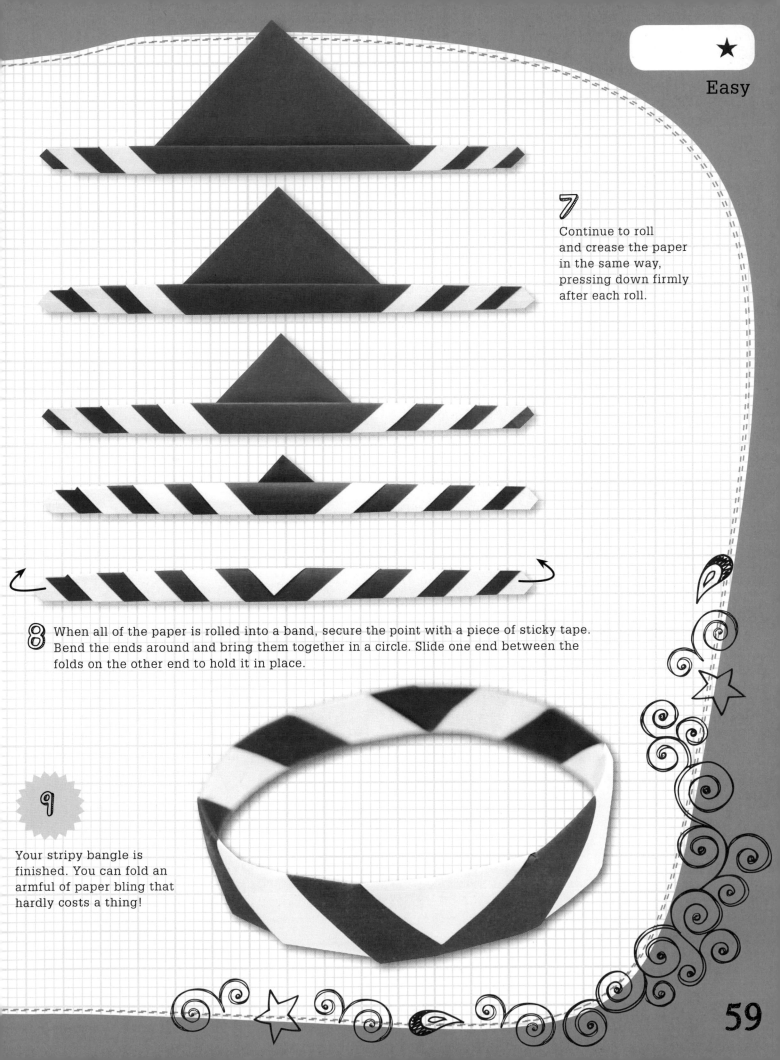

7 Continue to roll and crease the paper in the same way, pressing down firmly after each roll.

8 When all of the paper is rolled into a band, secure the point with a piece of sticky tape. Bend the ends around and bring them together in a circle. Slide one end between the folds on the other end to hold it in place.

9 Your stripy bangle is finished. You can fold an armful of paper bling that hardly costs a thing!

59

Socks

Don't worry about odd socks on paper washing day. Fold lots of pairs, pin them on a line, and watch them flutter in the breeze for fun!

1 Place the paper as shown. Fold it in half from top to bottom and unfold, then from left to right and unfold.

2 Make creases on either side, 45 mm (1¾ in) from the points, and fold in the corners.

3 Turn the paper over.

4 Make a crease at the bottom corner around 30 mm (1½ in) from the point and fold in.

5 Valley fold a 15 mm (¾ in) section on the left and right edges. Make sure the creases are straight.

6 Make a new crease across the top as shown and fold down the corner.

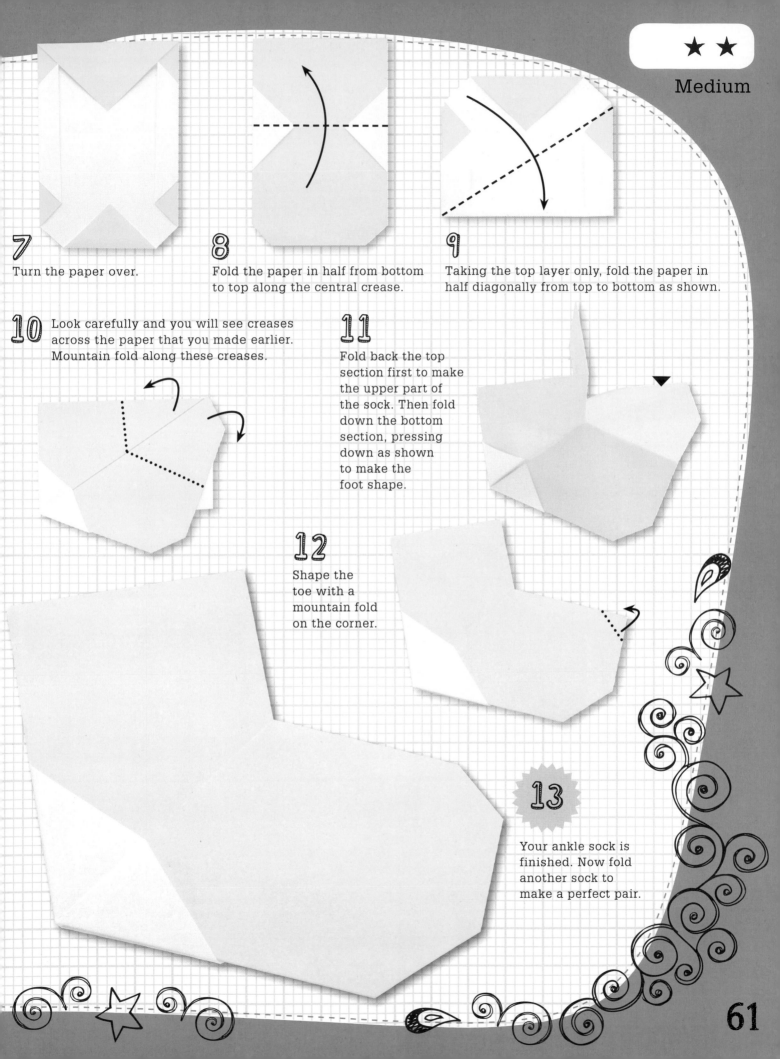

7 Turn the paper over.

8 Fold the paper in half from bottom to top along the central crease.

9 Taking the top layer only, fold the paper in half diagonally from top to bottom as shown.

10 Look carefully and you will see creases across the paper that you made earlier. Mountain fold along these creases.

11 Fold back the top section first to make the upper part of the sock. Then fold down the bottom section, pressing down as shown to make the foot shape.

12 Shape the toe with a mountain fold on the corner.

13 Your ankle sock is finished. Now fold another sock to make a perfect pair.

Boots

Footwear doesn't need to be black or brown. Be bold with red, yellow, or blue, and fold some trendy heeled boots topped with white trim.

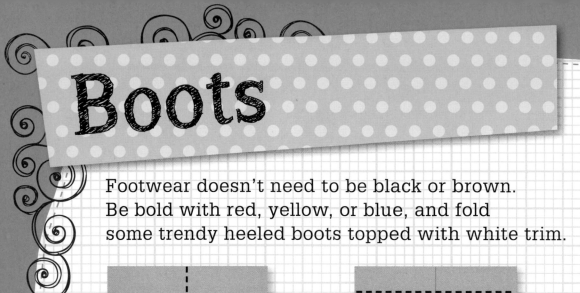

1
Fold the paper from left to right and unfold, then from top to bottom and unfold.

2
Make a crease around 25 mm (1 in) from the top edge and fold the paper over.

3
Turn the paper over.

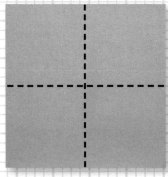

4
Fold the left and right edges in to meet the central crease.

5
On the top layer, make a crease from the middle point to the bottom right corner.

6
Fold the paper over along the crease. Now unfold the left-hand side.

7
Valley fold the paper from the central crease on the left edge to the right edge as shown.

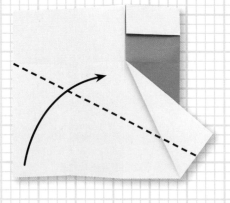

8
Fold over the left side along the crease you made in step 4. Make a diagonal fold from the bottom of this crease to the right edge, just above the central crease, then unfold.

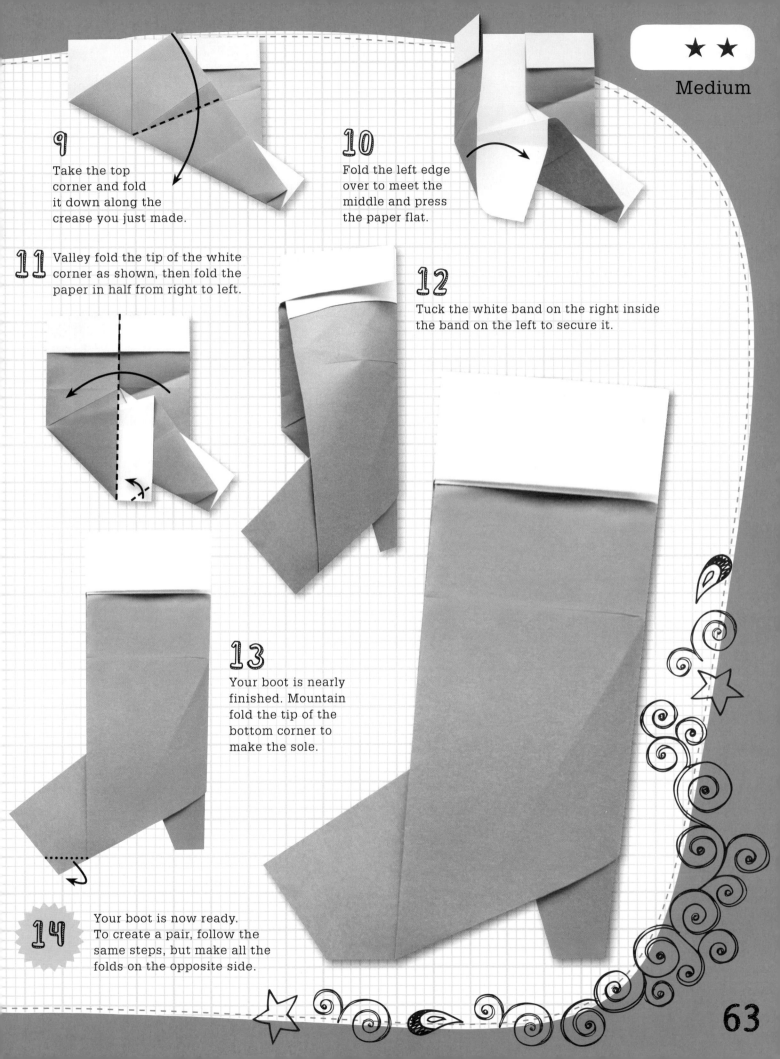

9 Take the top corner and fold it down along the crease you just made.

10 Fold the left edge over to meet the middle and press the paper flat.

11 Valley fold the tip of the white corner as shown, then fold the paper in half from right to left.

12 Tuck the white band on the right inside the band on the left to secure it.

13 Your boot is nearly finished. Mountain fold the tip of the bottom corner to make the sole.

14 Your boot is now ready. To create a pair, follow the same steps, but make all the folds on the opposite side.

63

Mittens

It takes some clever folding to create a pair of cosy mittens. Make a beanie hat to match the mitts and you are all ready for a paper snowball fight!

1 Fold the paper in half from top to bottom and unfold. Then from left to right and unfold.

2 Fold the paper in half again from right to left.

3 Taking the top layer only, fold the left edge over to meet the right edge.

4 Make a diagonal crease from the bottom corner as shown. Make another crease that meets it in a 'V', then unfold both creases.

5 Take the bottom right corner and pull it up and to the side. Press down on the upper edge, as shown, to make a new crease.

6 Flatten the paper to start off the thumb shape. Now fold down the corner as shown.

7 When you have this shape, open up the paper a little and pull down the corner slightly. Press flat to crease.

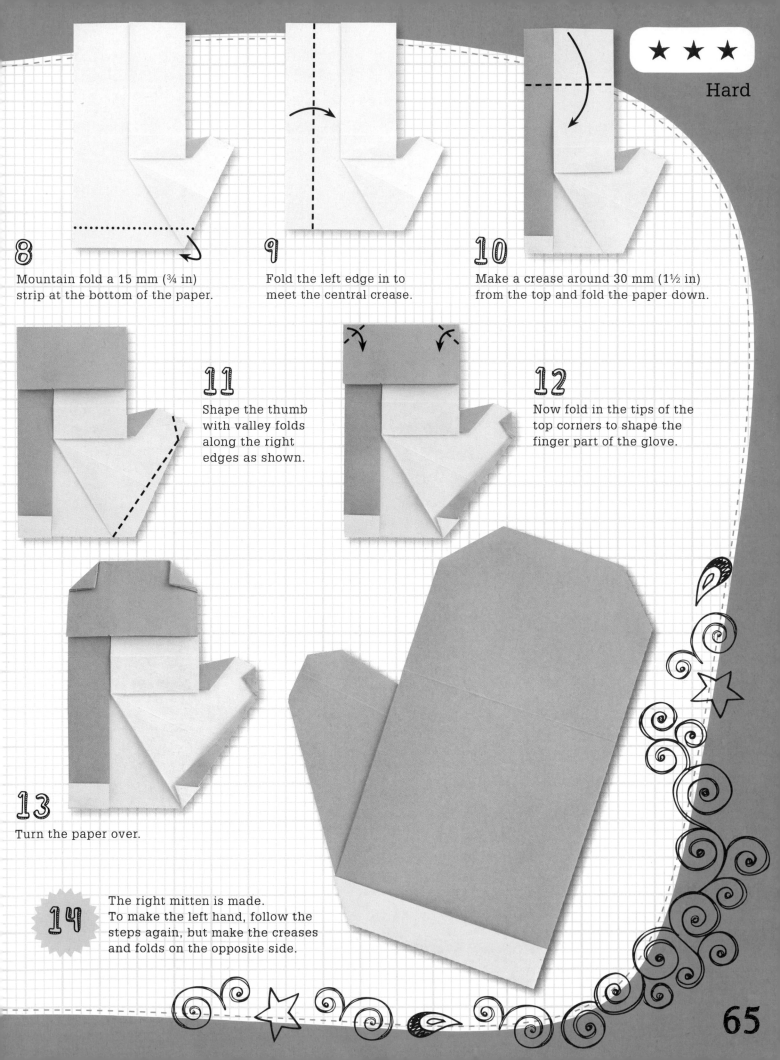

★ ★ ★

Hard

8

Mountain fold a 15 mm (¾ in) strip at the bottom of the paper.

9

Fold the left edge in to meet the central crease.

10

Make a crease around 30 mm (1½ in) from the top and fold the paper down.

11

Shape the thumb with valley folds along the right edges as shown.

12

Now fold in the tips of the top corners to shape the finger part of the glove.

13

Turn the paper over.

14

The right mitten is made. To make the left hand, follow the steps again, but make the creases and folds on the opposite side.

Hats

When it comes to folded fashions, hats are hip! Find out how to make a host of headgear, from an easy-peasy beanie to a Stetson straight out of the Wild West.

Cowboy hat

Howdy partner!

Here comes the King!

Crown

Beanie

Pixie hat

Alakazam!

Wizard's hat

67

Beanie

A beanie is the perfect hat to keep your ears warm in cold weather. It's so simple to fold you can make a different one for every day of the week.

1 Fold the paper in half from top to bottom.

2 Make a crease in the left corner. Fold it over, making sure the edges are straight.

3 Fold over the right corner, making sure its bottom edge lines up with the one on the left.

4 Now make the hat band. Taking the top layer, fold in the bottom edge just under the folded corners.

5 Now mountain fold the lower layer to complete the hat band.

6 Fold in the left-hand point. Crease firmly.

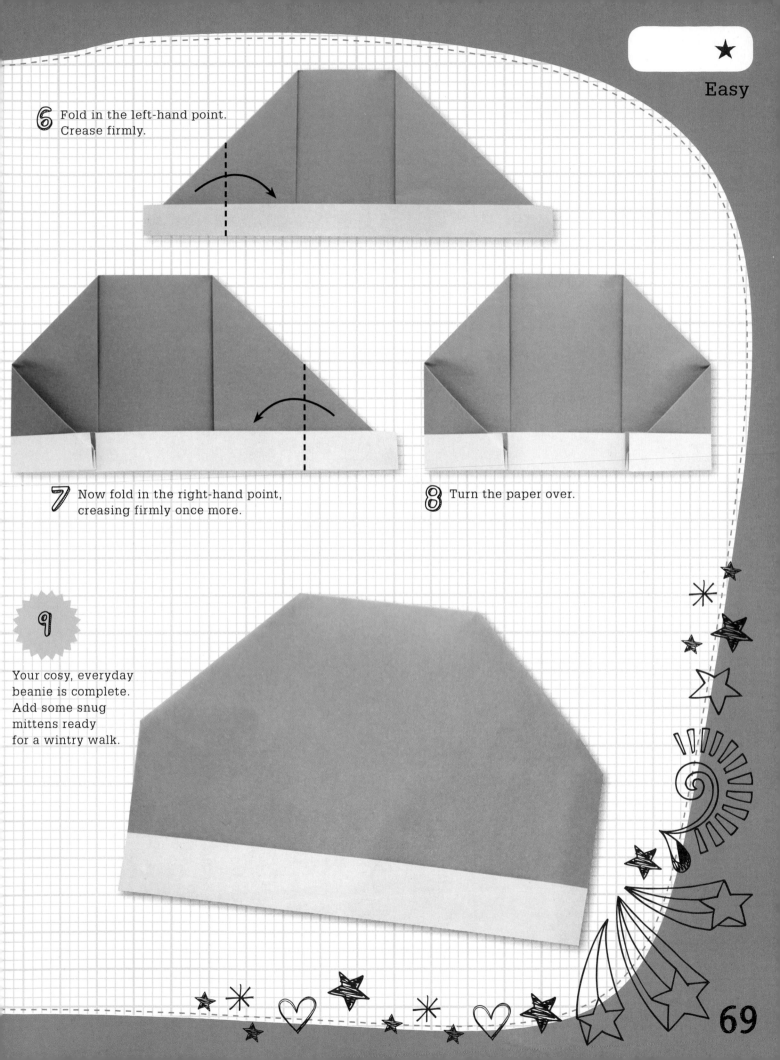

7 Now fold in the right-hand point, creasing firmly once more.

8 Turn the paper over.

9 Your cosy, everyday beanie is complete. Add some snug mittens ready for a wintry walk.

Crown

This fabulous crown is fit for a king or queen. Use yellow paper that glows like gold and it will sit proudly on any royal head.

1 Place the paper as shown. Fold in half from left to right.

2 Fold in the left and right corners to meet the central crease.

3 Fold in the top and bottom corners in the same way.

4 You should now have a square. Turn the paper over.

5 Fold over the top edge to meet the central crease.

6 Repeat with the bottom edge.

7 Fold in the bottom triangle so the white side is showing.

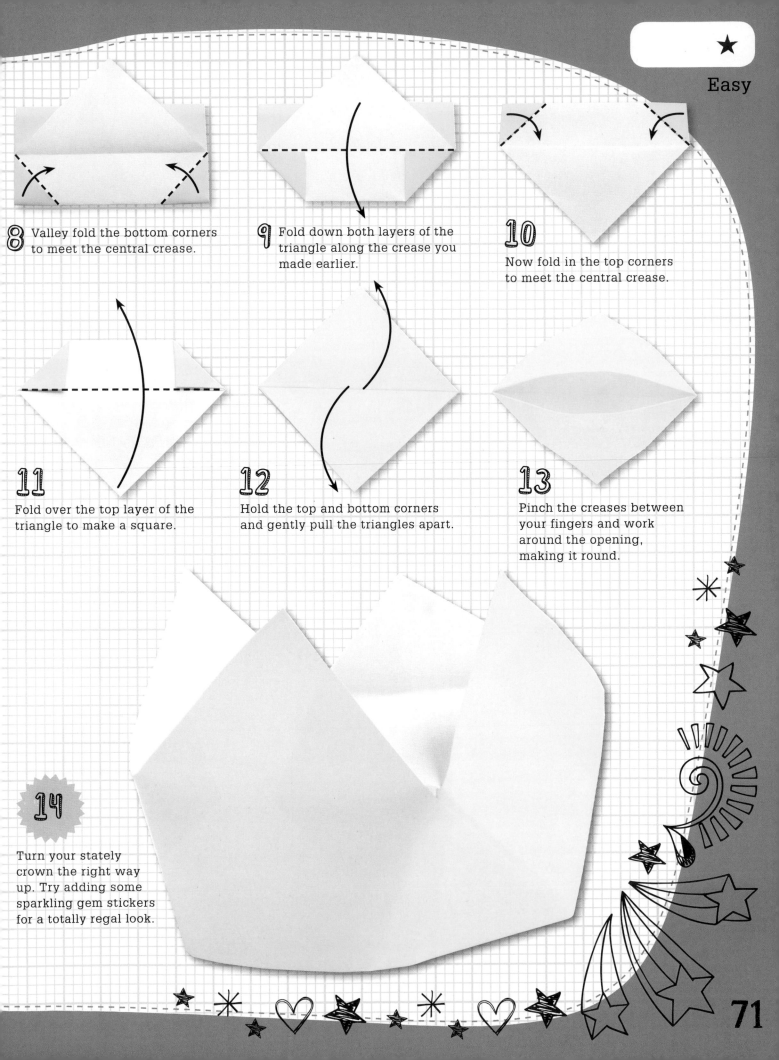

8 Valley fold the bottom corners to meet the central crease.

9 Fold down both layers of the triangle along the crease you made earlier.

10 Now fold in the top corners to meet the central crease.

11 Fold over the top layer of the triangle to make a square.

12 Hold the top and bottom corners and gently pull the triangles apart.

13 Pinch the creases between your fingers and work around the opening, making it round.

14 Turn your stately crown the right way up. Try adding some sparkling gem stickers for a totally regal look.

Wizard's hat

Take a square of paper and conjure up a wizard's pointy hat. You don't need special powers, just a little paper-folding magic!

1 Place the paper as shown and fold it in half from top to bottom.

2 Fold it in half from left to right and unfold.

3 Fold in the top points to meet the bottom point. This makes a square.

4 Fold in the left and right edges from the top corner to meet the central crease. This makes a kite shape.

5 Taking the top layers only, fold in the bottom triangles.

6 Make two angled creases that meet in a 'V'. Fold over so that the points meet the outer edges.

7 Taking the top layer only, fold in the bottom triangle as shown.

8 Fold in the top layer once more to line up with the bottom of the hat.

9 Take the remaining triangle and tuck it up inside the hat. Now open up the hat slightly so it stands up on its own.

10 Your hat is ready for some hocus pocus. Draw on some stars and moons for extra pizzazz.

Pixie hat

You could make some mischief with this enchanting pixie hat. Fold it carefully from forest green paper and leave it out for a little person to find!

1 Place the paper as shown and fold it in half from bottom to top.

2 Fold the paper in half from left to right, then unfold.

3 Fold over the left corner. The point should touch the right-hand edge and the top edge should be straight.

4 Repeat with the right corner. The top edges should overlap and line up.

5 Make a crease just above the folded corners. Fold over the top layer of the top corner.

6 Mountain fold the bottom layer.

7 You now have a paper cup. Turn the cup upside down.

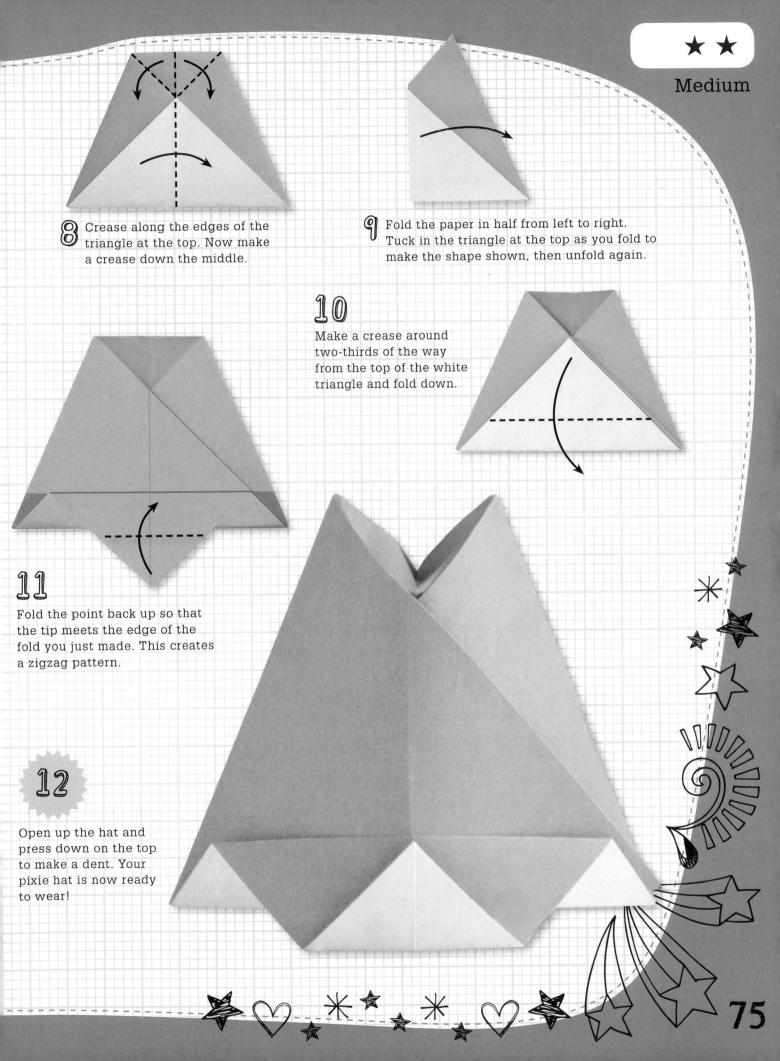

8 Crease along the edges of the triangle at the top. Now make a crease down the middle.

9 Fold the paper in half from left to right. Tuck in the triangle at the top as you fold to make the shape shown, then unfold again.

10 Make a crease around two-thirds of the way from the top of the white triangle and fold down.

11 Fold the point back up so that the tip meets the edge of the fold you just made. This creates a zigzag pattern.

12 Open up the hat and press down on the top to make a dent. Your pixie hat is now ready to wear!

Cowboy hat

No cowboy is complete without his Stetson. It keeps out the sun and the rain on long rides across the prairies, and it looks seriously cool!

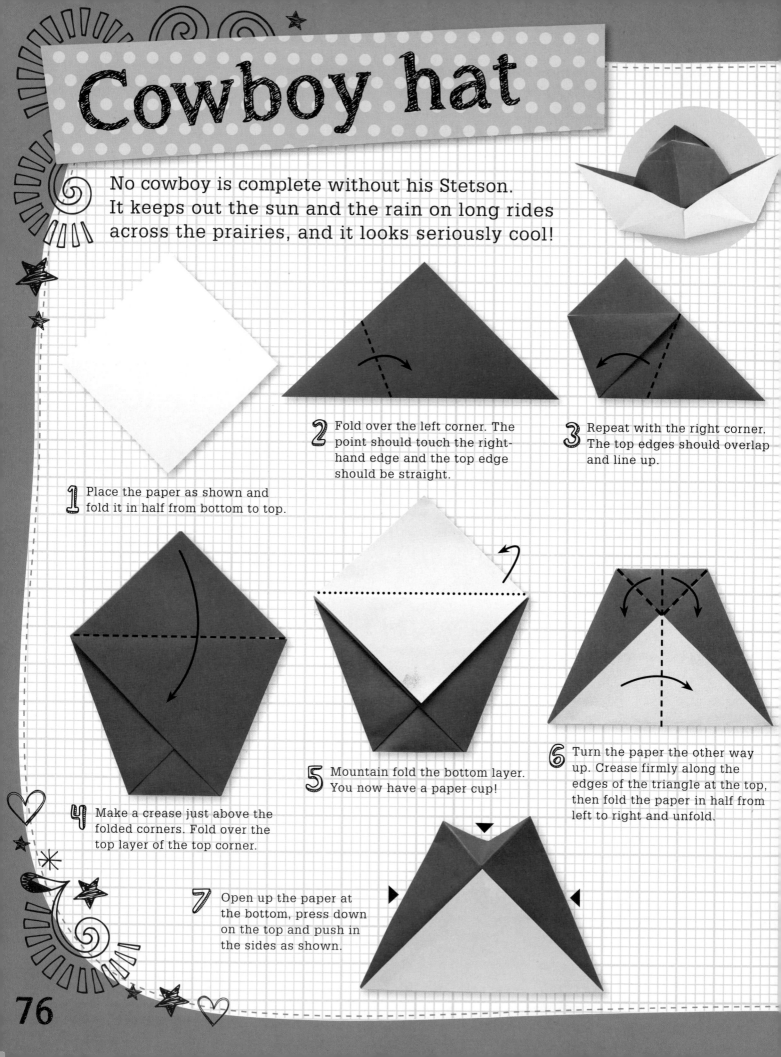

1 Place the paper as shown and fold it in half from bottom to top.

2 Fold over the left corner. The point should touch the right-hand edge and the top edge should be straight.

3 Repeat with the right corner. The top edges should overlap and line up.

4 Make a crease just above the folded corners. Fold over the top layer of the top corner.

5 Mountain fold the bottom layer. You now have a paper cup!

6 Turn the paper the other way up. Crease firmly along the edges of the triangle at the top, then fold the paper in half from left to right and unfold.

7 Open up the paper at the bottom, press down on the top and push in the sides as shown.

8 Your paper should look like this. Take the top layer of the bottom point and fold it in.

9 Now mountain fold the bottom layer.

10 Gently pull down the white paper layer on either side. Flatten out the bottom edges.

11 Open up the hat so it stands up on its own.

12 Your cowboy hat is ready to hit the trail. Saddle up your trusty horse and head off into the sunset. Yee-ha!

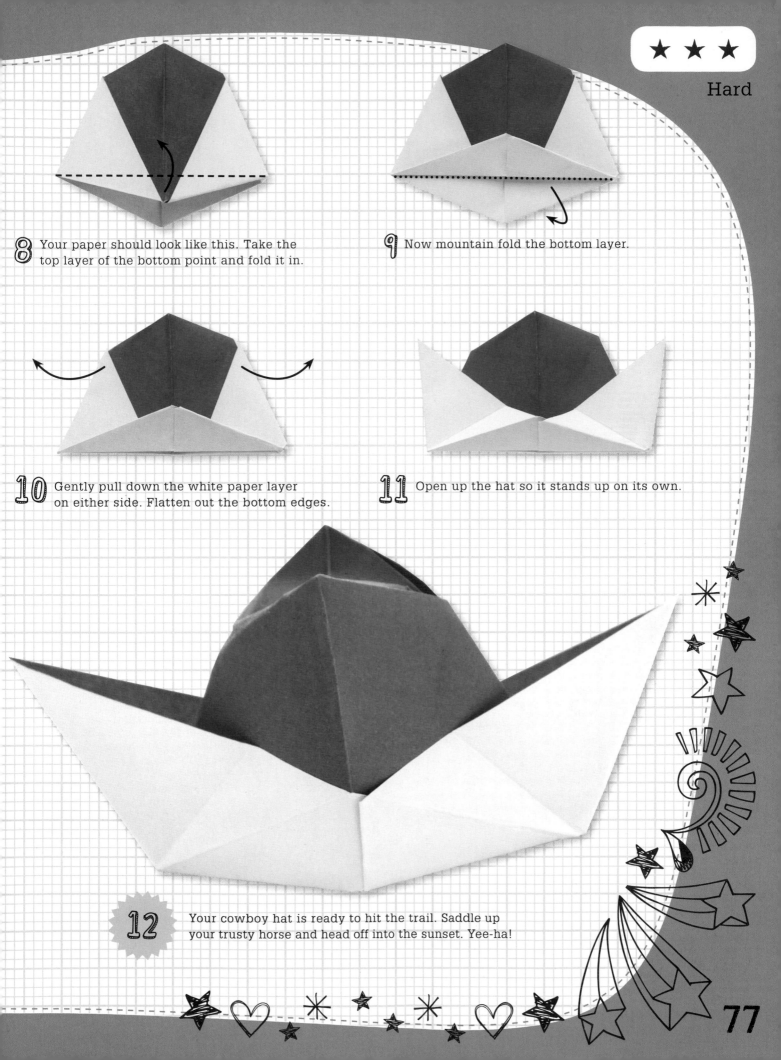

Special outfits

There's an outfit to fold for every occasion, whether it's a special ceremony, a dazzling wedding, or just a day at work.

Uniform

Here comes the bride!

Wedding dress

Kimono

Apron

Mmm, what's cooking?

Cheerleader

Go team, go!

79

Uniform

Fold a smart uniform that works for lots of jobs, from a nurse to an air stewardess. Master the steps and you can kit out a whole workforce!

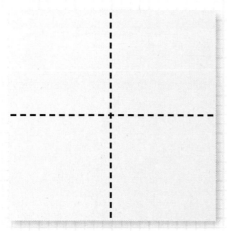

1 Fold the paper from top to bottom and unfold. Then from left to right and unfold.

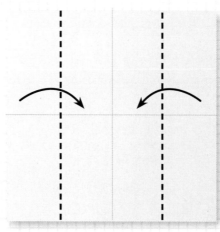

2 Fold the edges in to meet the central crease.

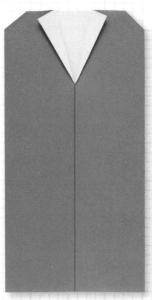

3 To make the collar, mak two angled creases that meet in a 'V' as shown.

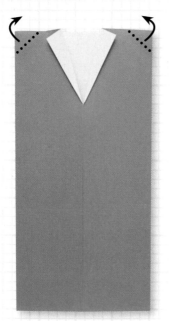

4 Shape the shoulders by mountain folding the tip of the top corners.

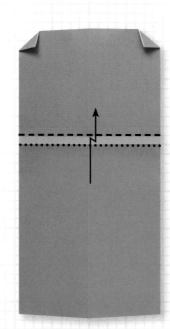

5 Turn the paper over.

6 Make the waist with a step fold across the middle of the paper.

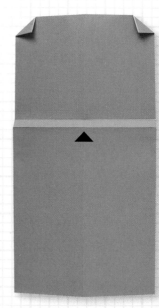

7 Press down on the step fold so that it lies flat.

8 Now to shape the waist. First make an angled crease on the lower section.

9 Pinch the corner between your fingers as shown and fold it over. Press down firmly on the edge of the upper section to crease.

10 Repeat on the other side.

11

Turn the paper over to see the finished dress.

12 You now have a neat and tidy uniform ready for duty! Will it be for a nurse to wear on the wards, or a high-flying stewardess to take to the skies?

Cheerleader

This fun cheerleader dress is a real crowd-pleaser. Pick a bright paper that will really stand out on the pitch and prepare to make some noise!

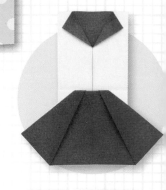

1 Fold the paper from top to bottom and unfold. Then from left to right and unfold.

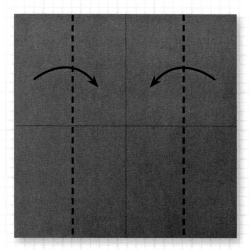

2 Fold the edges in to meet the central crease.

3 Make the skirt by folding over the bottom edges as shown.

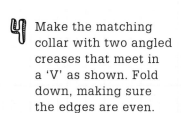

4 Make the matching collar with two angled creases that meet in a 'V' as shown. Fold down, making sure the edges are even.

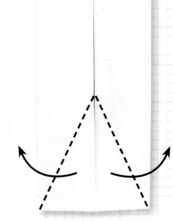

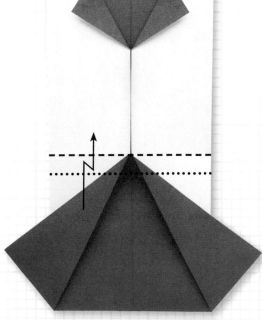

5 Create the waist with a step fold. Start with a valley fold across the central crease.

6 Press down on the step fold so that it lies flat.

7 Mountain fold 5 mm (¼ in) from the edge on either side, keeping the sides straight.

8 Now your eye-catching cheerleader dress is ready for action! Entertain the crowds with some rousing routines and cheer your team on to victory!

Wedding dress

This gorgeous white gown is every bride's dream. With some careful folding you can create a beautiful bodice and a sweeping skirt to make the groom gasp!

1 Fold the paper from top to bottom and unfold. Then from left to right and unfold.

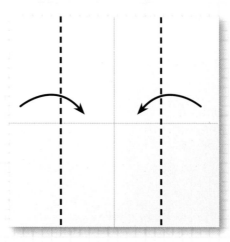

2 Fold the edges in to meet the central crease.

3 Fold the edges in to meet the central crease once more.

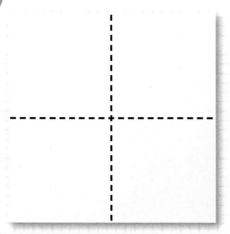

4 Completely unfold the paper. Turn the paper over.

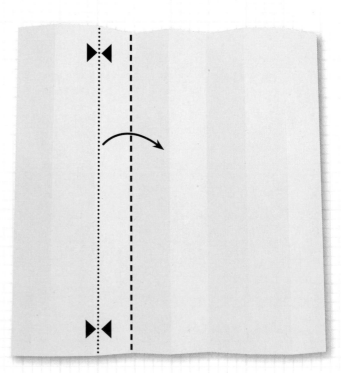

5 Now make a pleat. Take the second crease from the left to meet the central crease. Press flat.

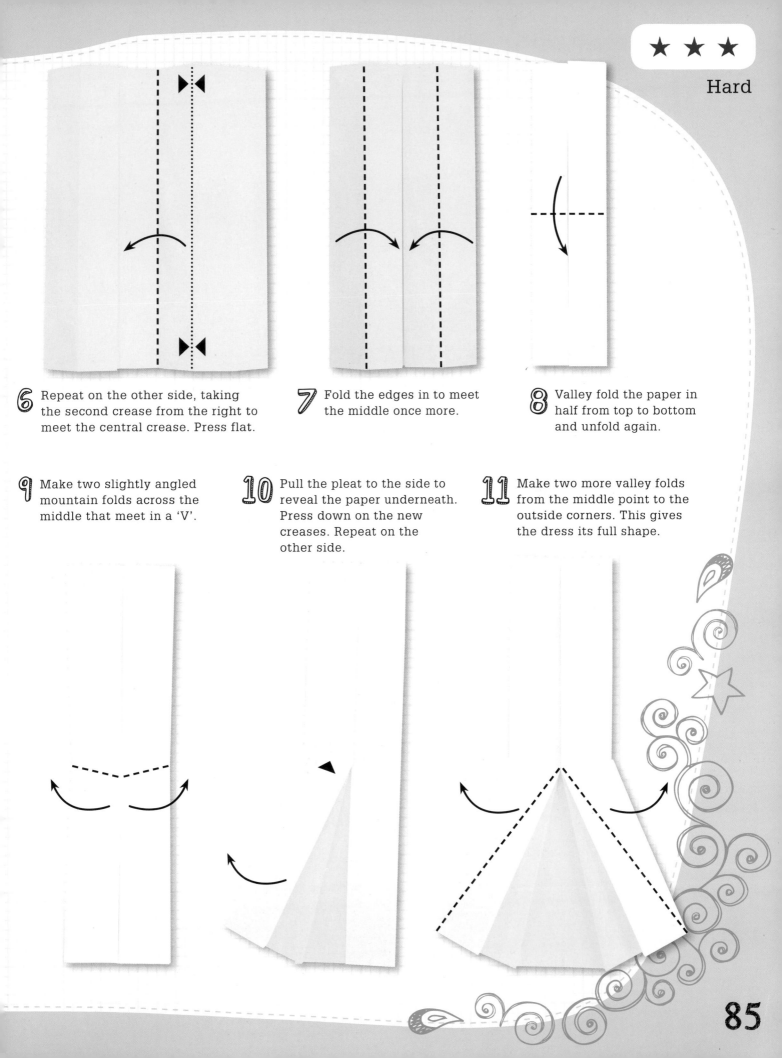

6 Repeat on the other side, taking the second crease from the right to meet the central crease. Press flat.

7 Fold the edges in to meet the middle once more.

8 Valley fold the paper in half from top to bottom and unfold again.

9 Make two slightly angled mountain folds across the middle that meet in a 'V'.

10 Pull the pleat to the side to reveal the paper underneath. Press down on the new creases. Repeat on the other side.

11 Make two more valley folds from the middle point to the outside corners. This gives the dress its full shape.

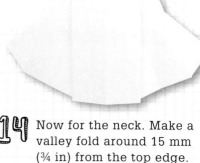

12 Make two angled creases from the top corners that meet in a 'V' as shown.

13 Fold along these creases to make the sleeve shapes. Turn the paper over.

14 Now for the neck. Make a valley fold around 15 mm (¾ in) from the top edge.

15 Put your finger on the lower layer of the pleat. Press down on the creases on either side to flatten them into triangular shapes.

16 Now open up the neck with two angled mountain folds as shown.

17 Valley fold the bottom edge of the neck to neaten it up.

18

Create the waist with a step fold. Start with a valley fold across the central crease.

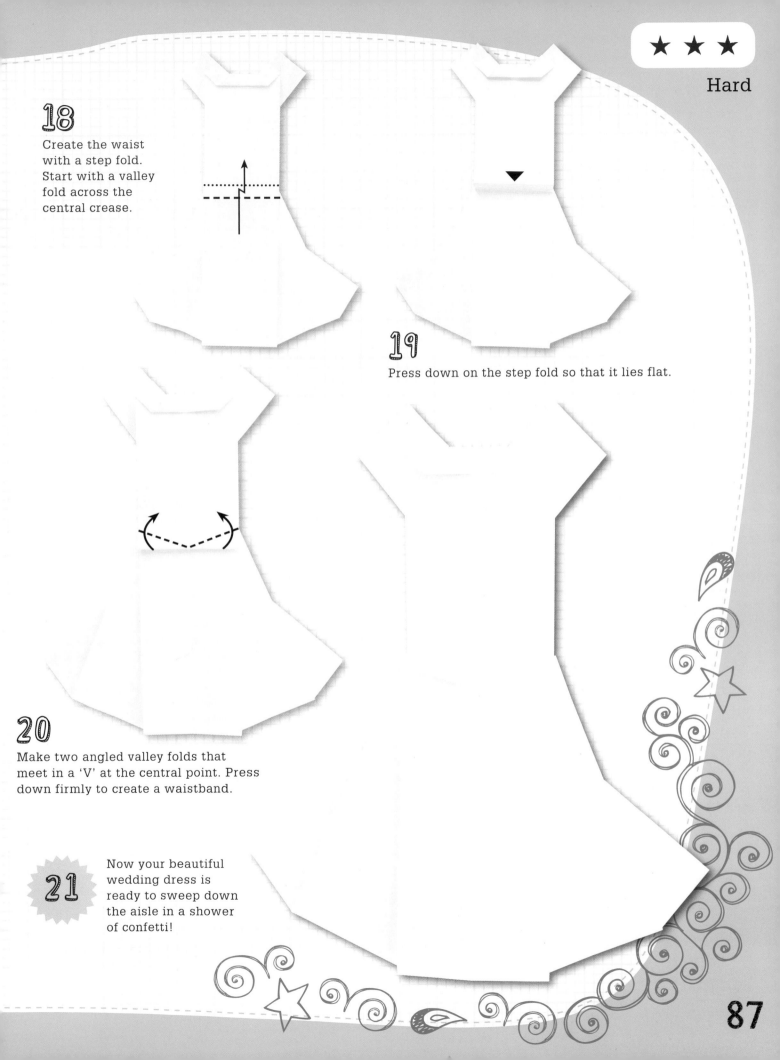

19

Press down on the step fold so that it lies flat.

20

Make two angled valley folds that meet in a 'V' at the central point. Press down firmly to create a waistband.

21 Now your beautiful wedding dress is ready to sweep down the aisle in a shower of confetti!

Kimono

Follow the steps to turn an ordinary square of paper into an amazing, oriental robe. Deep red is the perfect shade for this traditional Japanese costume.

1

Fold the paper in half from left to right and unfold.

2

Fold the edges in to meet the central crease.

3

Unfold the paper and turn it over.

4

Now make a pleat. Take the first crease on the left to meet the central crease. Press flat.

5

Repeat on the other side, taking the first crease on the right to meet the central crease. Press flat.

6

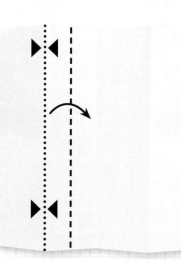

You should now have a pleat down the middle of the paper, like this.

8 Make a step fold as shown. When it is pressed flat, the step fold should touch the paper just below the folded top edge.

7 Make a valley fold about 10 mm (½ in) from the top edge.

9 Make the collar by opening up the pleat at the top. Put your finger on the lower layer, then press down on the creases on either side to flatten them into triangular shapes.

10 Make a step fold in the top half of the collar.

11 Make a crease down the left side from the edge of the collar.

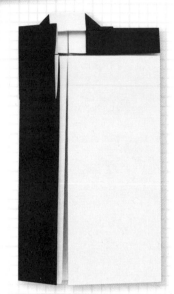

12 Fold firmly along the new crease and unfold again.

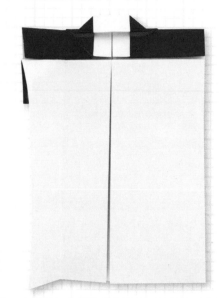

13 To make the first sleeve, open up the corner of the lower section.

14 Push down on the crease that runs along the top and press it flat, folding in the edge of the paper as you go.

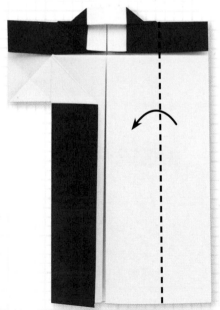

15 Now make a crease down the right side from the edge of the collar.

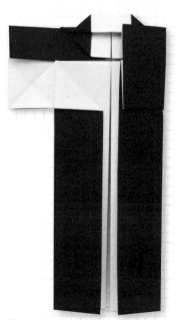

16 Fold firmly along the new crease, then unfold again.

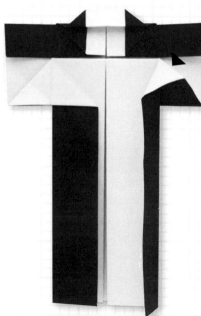

17 Open up the corner, as before, and press it flat to make the other sleeve.

18 Make an angled crease below the sleeve, as shown, and fold over.

19 Crease and fold the right-hand side in the same way to make the flared robe.

20 Valley fold the tips of the sleeves.

21 Turn the paper over to see the finished garment.

22 Take a bow! Your Japanese kimono is ready for a special occasion, like a tea ceremony or a wedding.

Apron

Roll up your sleeves and prepare for some fancy folding to create this pretty apron. All you need are nimble fingers and a square of paper!

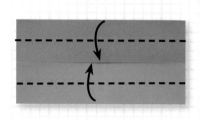

1 Fold the paper from top to bottom and unfold. Then from left to right and unfold.

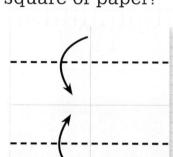

2 Fold the top and bottom edges in to meet the central crease.

3 Fold the top and bottom edges in to meet the central crease once more.

4 Open up the paper.

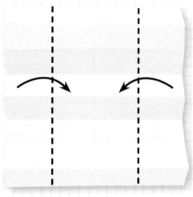

5 With the creases running across, fold the left and right edges in to meet the central crease.

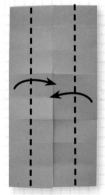

6 Repeat once more, folding the edges in to meet the central crease.

7 Open up the paper and you will see the checked pattern of creases.

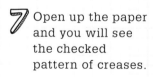

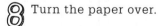

8 Turn the paper over.

9 Fold in the left edge to meet the first crease. Repeat on the other side.

10 Now fold up the bottom edge to meet the first crease from the bottom.

11 Turn the paper over.

12 Fold in the sides along the second crease from each edge.

13 Turn the paper over.

14 Fold down the top edge along the first crease.

15 To make the neck, open up the top left corner and press down on the crease to flatten it into a triangular shape. Repeat on the other side.

Apron

16 Make the waist with a step fold across the middle of the dress.

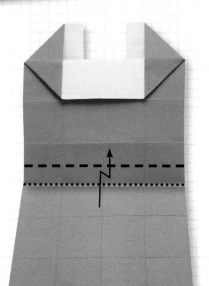

17 Press down on the step fold so that it lies flat.

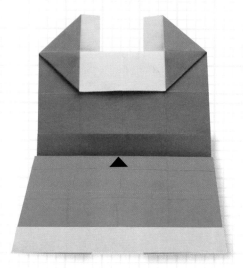

18 Make two angled creases at the corners of the step fold as shown.

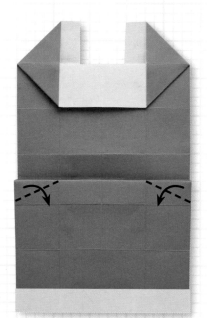

19 Fold and crease firmly, then unfold.

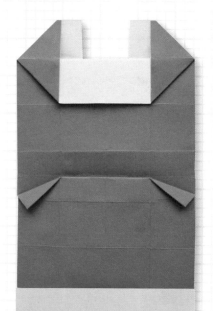

20 Turn the paper over.

21 Valley fold the upper left edge to meet the central crease.

22 The lower section will be pulled across. Press down on it to make an angled crease.

23 Repeat on the right. Fold in the upper edge and press down on the lower section to make an angled crease.

24 Make two final angled valley folds at the top, as shown. Turn the paper over.

25 Your apron is ready for some making, baking, icing, and spicing. Don't worry about splashes and spills, you can always fold another one!

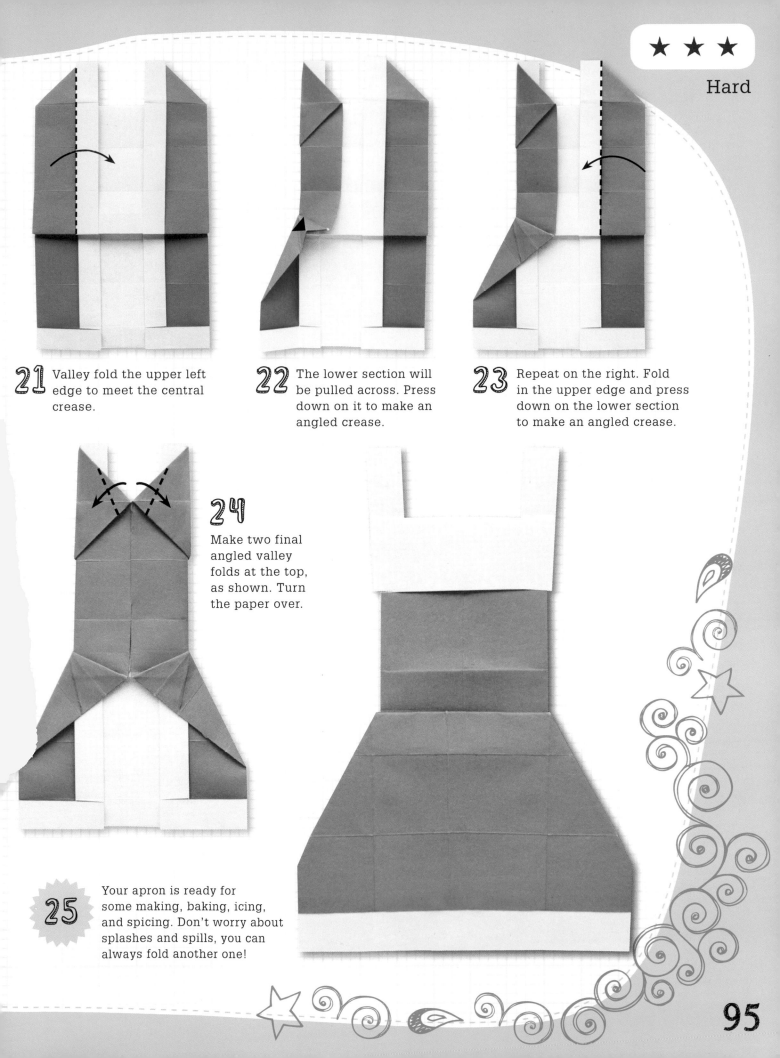

Now you have created a fabulous collection of paper clothes, have a go at being a top fashion stylist. Put together some gorgeous outfits to suit every occasion.

Mix and match tops, skirts, and shorts, try out shoes and hats, then throw in some cute accessories to complete each look!

Party on

Look smart

Wrap up

Stay cool